THE
FRENC
FOREIGN
LEGION

By Georges D'Esparbes

1901

2018 Translation by Matthew Lynch

PREFACE

In presenting to the public this work on the modern Foreign Legion as I saw it within the short space of a month, I take for granted that such a study will be called incomplete. I was not able to interview many of the individuals I wished to, and of course I could not get the most aloof and the most violent souls of the Legion to open their hearts to me. I did not do all, but I did what I could. It would have been simple to write something superficial on the topic, but the readers to whom this book is addressed would not have forgiven me for it, as they are looking for a solid base of documentation. Therefore I have proceeded in the following manner: I gave no thought to relying upon hearsay to frame my impressions. What I saw I recorded, and I wrote down only what was said to me. Imagination would have led my book astray and so destroyed its value, which is its sincerity.

THE FOREIGN LEGION

The day of my arrival at Bel–Abbès I was presented to lieutenant B… , an amicable blond soldier who had performed brilliantly at Tonkin.

"I am told, Lieutenant," said I, "that you were chosen to write a history of the Legion. I expect some words regarding its past would be of interest to the public. Does the Legion date back to the conquest of Algeria?"

"That is the time of its definitive creation," said the Lieutenant, "but to truly understand you must look further back. It is generally held that the Legion is a wholly modern institution, but it has existed in some form for centuries, and is still in use today for many of the same reasons. Is it the lack of citizens willing to go to war, or perhaps the need for France to win at all costs that constitutes the success of the Foreign Legion? I leave it to you to decide. My task is only to arrange the various feats of arms performed by the Legion in chronological order, following its various transformations throughout the years. This book is then to be distributed to the men."

"I want to know more," said I, "about your mercenary past. Since you are steeped in the lore, Lieutenant, I would like to speak with you about it for a time, as you are so familiar…"

We entered into the shadowy greenness of *Mascara Street* and Lieutenant M. B… sketched out in the simplest possible terms the history of the French Foreign Legion.

I was reminded of all of the well known facts and many others that are forgotten among the French populace. I was reminded of the Scottish guard of Charles VII, and the Swiss, the Albanians or *Stradiots*, the Flemish, the Walloons, the Germans or *Lansquenets*, the Irish, the Italians, the Corsicans, the Swedes, the English, and the Spaniards who had been employed by his successors.

"What motives gave rise to the routine use of foreign troops?"

"The independence of the nobility," he said, "compelled the Kings of France to make use of mercenary troops."

"The courage and devotion of these troops," he continued as we walked along, "made them a perfect fit for the needs of the various sovereigns. The Swiss Guard were in the same unit as the French Guard, and the One Hundred Swiss and the Scottish

Bodyguards were incorporated into the royal household."

"With the fall of the monarchy, the Convention called upon all of the peoples of Europe to defend France. The creation of the Foreign Legion really dates from the First Republic: At this point the government created the Batavian Legions along with the Allobrogians, the Italians, and the Poles."

"In Egypt, Bonaparte made use of the Greeks, Copts, and Mameluks. Under the Empire a host of foreigners rushed in, dazzled by French glory. Regiments of Swiss, Poles, Hanoverians, Irish, Portuguese, Spaniards, Albanians, Greeks, Croats, Illyrians, and Prussians were created once again. Three new regiments were formed to receive deserters from every nation. Belgians, Dutchmen, and Germans were incorporated into the national army."

"These groups were dissolved at the end of the Napoleonic Wars," added the Lieutenant, "but among these troops many had come to love France, and to retain these men Louis XVIII created a *Foreign Colonial Regiment.*"

"We then turned our attention to Tlemcen [Algeria] where disgruntled Moorish elements were making their presence felt."

"During the One Hundred Days Napoleon created eight foreign regiments. Louis XVIII dissolved them and created a Royal Foreign Legion in their place. This was the Legion of Hohenlohe which was called the 21st Light when it was dissolved."

"To conclude, the counter-coup of the Revolution of 1830 was felt throughout Europe, and many political outlaws came to seek refuge among our ranks. To make use of these nationless foreign militants the law of the 9th of May 1831 created the the Foreign Legion which could only be used on foreign soil, as Mr. les Chambres doubted the loyalty of such mercenaries."

"Who is les Chambres?"

"A politician," said the soldier coldly, "who had it in for foreign troops, despite the fact that they had had nothing to do with the political unrest of that time."

"He was an honest enough figure, never batting an eyelash at anything. I have read about his melancholic and passive virtues: Silence, stoicism, a defense of the existing order, tight-lipped enthusiasm, discipline. And with all of this he spoke of us as an anti-social army and a military peril."

"The army consisted at first of 7 battalions of 8 companies each. The men were divided into battalions by nationality: The 1st, 2nd, and 3rd were

Swiss and German, the 4th was Spanish, the 5th was Italian, the 6th was Belgian and Dutch, and the 7th was Polish. These left for Algeria in 1831, and the modern Legion was born. And here I am at the end of my little course," joked the officer with a smile, "you will learn the rest from speaking to my comrades or by observation. What are you doing this morning?"

"I'm going to have a glass at the Moorish Cafe."

"That's good. Drink quickly and go stand watch at the train station. Thirty or so recruits are coming from Oran. You'll see, it is sometimes very entertaining, there are some real characters."

I went to the station where I met with another young lieutenant, an elegant little man of few words. He was an ex-alpine officer who had come to Algeria for a change of scenery.

"Are you here to meet the greenhorns?" he asked.

"Like you perhaps, Lieutenant."

"Yes, I like to see them here first, rather than back at the barracks. Without them paying attention you have the leisure to watch so that you know what you will be dealing with later on – one can avoid mistakes in this way. Our tailors fit them all with the same uniform, but each of these men has his particular angles. And then," he added in a lower tone, "I admit that I have fun with it, as there is an exercise in psychology I like to perform which is not included in the regulations. Let's step back, here comes the train."

A few moments later the detachment appeared behind a Legion noncom. Upon seeing us, a tall skinny recruit without his hat stepped down onto the platform while burying a half-smoked cigar in his pocket.

"A Frenchman," said the Lieutenant, "I'd even wager he's from Bat' d'Af."

Bel-Abbès Mosque. (Parade ground.)

The group of twenty-six men stopped behind the sergeant who ordered them to form up by fours with a motion of his hand. I looked over the recruits and gazed into their faces.

Some expressed nothing while others wanted nothing to be expressed. On the whole they gave me the impression of being featureless like closed casks where you can only guess at the contents, be it gems or dust. A little man wearing a tattered pink kerchief had his right arm in a sling, and through the corporal we learned that he had fought at Dole. The two youngest men were honest-looking blondes who seemed a bit bewildered. They barely had facial hair and they were timid. They had three comrades from Alsace and Lorraine. While the noncom counted the men with one eye on his list, the corporal laughed as he looked at them. He indicated to us a man we had not yet seen, and who seemed to be hiding. The recruit had a full beard, his eyes were way up over by his ears like a calf, and he was still carrying a riding crop and wearing a jockey's helmet. He was wearing a white linen tunic with a brown jacket, and the tunic came down like a skirt to reveal his black legs stuffed into tattered slippers. We knew full well that he had gambled with his pants away immediately after coming to Fort Saint-Jean in Marseille.

"Helbreiner!"

"Present!"

"Fosse!"

"Present!"

We drew a bit closer and I could see them in full measure as the sun highlighted their least flaws to reveal what poverty can do to the human body. Their faces were just a mass of features, and their shattered nerves no longer allowed these to obey the commands of emotion. Among this mass of the downtrodden was a big brown man with a massive jaw who looked at the town with a satisfied air.

"Ah," said the Lieutenant, "great hands, that one is a true Legionnaire. An adventurer, a man of action, you see how impatient he seems?"

After this I saw two doglike eyes watching me which were soft, deep, and fixed. I turned to the corporal and asked: "Who is that fellow?"

He glanced at his roster and said: "A Bulgarian who wept a lot on the boat. But he's not the only foreigner. We have four Belgians, a Swiss, a Bavarian noncom, two Spaniards, and an American, which is rare."

"Hermann!"

"Present."

"Mosso!"

"Present!"

"Agarta!"

"Present!"

"Hansen!"

"Present."

"Rivaux!"

"No Rivaux?" asked the noncom.

"Present!" shouted a heap of rags suddenly.

"Listen buddy," said the sergeant, "at the barracks you'd better open your ears and remember your name."

"He's one of the name-changers." the corporal said, "there's a whole bunch of them who do it."

"Deblander!"

"Present!"

"F…!"

"Present." murmured one individual who was sitting on the edge of the sidewalk behind the others. He suddenly loomed up above the rest of them like a mystery.

Hardly had I seen the man than I conceived a liking for him. As I watched him fixedly my other thoughts vanished like smoke and impressions of him rushed in on my mind like a disorderly mob. This unknown person presented my brain with too many riddles to guess at, and so he frightened and fascinated me even though he did not look at me, and it can only be on his surface that I base my imprudent judgements of him. I escorted the detachment, fascinated.

He was a man of thirty-five or thirty-eight with a somewhat ruddy complexion. His eyes were rather small and opaque, but there was an intelligence that dwelt in them, and the opaqueness was without a doubt apparent rather than real. His temples were close-shaved and gray, he had a strong chin, a full light-colored mustache, and a blood-blister on the left side of his nose. He was big and his cold gaze was firm as it rested upon the ground. The collar of his overcoat was raised on one side, and his shirtfront rumpled as if from a fight, sticking through his black vest at the point where a button was missing. His pants were clean and his boots were new. In the pocket of his overcoat he had a package wrapped in a big handkerchief which he had apparently borrowed from his companions. He walked with a long stride like a sportsman, sometimes striking the heels of the man in front of him. His dull and dirty cap was coming apart at the seams, and it had often been used to cover this forehead so heavy with life's misfortunes.

The lieutenant was no longer there. After taking a few steps I felt stupefied, and I experienced a sort of frenzy of pity. Where did he escape from, with his overcoat and his rubbishy silk hat? Was it from a dive bar? From woman troubles? Gambling? Which particular kind of hell? And here he was on the way to the barracks because he had been told it was like a monastery of action, a way to end it all faster, just like all of these other pilgrims.

No more fancy dinners, no more gazing at soft bare shoulders, no more flowers to buy, another existence entirely: The canteen, the rifle, the ship, the fever, or a bullet. After all, it might be his fault. What might his tender hands have done? What sobs had passed under that mustache? What brawl marked that nose?

Did you fight for money on the Rue Royale in the old port of Marseille? Did you lose your fortune at the track? Were you a wanted man? Were you…

Maybe you're just one more heart in ruins. One more disillusioned lover. Anonymous and full of suffering, hardly alive in your despair, you made a mistake and wept for it. So full of regret that you fled without taking a change of clothes after some terrible *event.*

And here we are, on the Rue de Daya, and here you are at the barracks. Well then, my suicidal friends, good luck! Here's the Legion's ticket office, one way to Madagascar, or Vietnam if there's no room, or Dahomey, or the south…

At noon I get the lowdown from the officers.

"The guy you mean," one of them said, "joined under the name of F… an Italian engineer. It may not be entirely untrue, but I have a Tuscan engineer who spoke with him, and our 'Italian' engineer hardly knows how to say hello."

"So who do you think he is?"

"Some man of the world who made mistakes, no doubt."

"And how do they fare?"

The officer understood the gist of my question and said:

"Those types are like the others: *they're heroes.*"

THE LIES

No inquiries are made regarding the declarations made by newcomers to the Legion:

"What's your name?"

The man invents a name.

"What age?"

He offers one.

"Profession?"

He writes whatever he wants to.

The officers who recruit them, de facto experts in 'experimental psychology', consider the shape of their heads for a moment, then shrug and say:

"Fourrier, conduct our recruits to the uniform station. Let's go, gentlemen."

This bit of politeness offered to the men who still bear the traces of intelligence on their faces is the last salute they will receive from civilized society. For those who come along already having left the world far behind, it is like an open door.

I have before me a roster prepared by a sergeant for my benefit. Here I can read the professions "announced" by those who entered the Legion from February to August of 1885, and from May to November 1898. I offer these to the reader in order to give a sense of the truth of the matter.

The total from these two semesters put together gives us 149 day-workers (manufacturing and farming), 103 office workers, 58 shoemakers, 56 fabric workers, 51 bakers, 49 locksmiths, 41 farmers, 37 students, 36 masons, 32 domestic servants, 32 accountants, 28 woodworkers, 26 miners, 25 butchers, 24 painters, 22 waiters, 21 stokers, 21 watchmakers, 20 gardeners, 20 blacksmiths, 19 mechanics, etc…

Many of these statistics, as you can guess, are the result of lies or imagination. Many a vulture has made himself out to be a monk in order to enter the ranks. An engineer will put himself down as a mechanic, the financier as a petty accountant, the architect as a construction worker, the notary a clerk, the industrialist as a factory hand, the nobleman a stable hand, the man of letters a gardener, the polymath a blacksmith, the scholar a farmer, and the business mogul a valet. The "no profession" column totals 112, and this is apparently full of ex-officers, doctors, professors, priests, and lawyers. It is the column of hidden misfortunes.

The nationality column provokes the same suspicions. I can read that within the space of two years, from 1896 to 1897, there were in the Legion in

Algeria some 2,635 men from Alsace and Lorraine, 2,511 Germans, 90 of which sought to become naturalized, 1,805 Frenchmen, 1,755 of which *signed on as foreigners.* There were 1,712 Belgians, 116 of which were naturalized, 975 Switzers, 87 of which were naturalized, 353 Austrians, 14 of which were naturalized, 81 Spaniards, 18 of which were naturalized, 56 Englishmen, 3 of which were naturalized (3 very extraordinary men), and 46 Turks, or self proclaimed Turks, who remained fiercely Turkish.

Should we accept the figures as they are? This table of the origins of the diverse elements of the Legion, set down for the years 1896–1897, presents us, upon reflection, with figures that we are obliged to interpret. In looking through them we can surmise some instinctive abandonments and adoptions: A certain number of Germans, for example, will declare that they are from Alsace, and some Austrians will do the same upon coming to the Legion. Many Frenchmen sign up as Swiss or Belgian, Spaniards and Italians swap places, and Romanians, Egyptians and Greeks become Turks. Why? Who knows… These lies cause one to think, for behind all of these tricks lies some deep well of mystery. Mr. Fourrier meets them in the office and poses his three questions without insisting upon the answers, as he has no cause to trip them up.

Thus everything is a lie in this crowd. Furthermore you could say that they live in an eternal state of dishonesty. They lie to themselves to maintain an illusion and they lie to one another to justify their various lies. They will lie about a comrade to maintain his status no matter how horrible his fault, and the most terrible past will be heaped under lies until the truth is annihilated. But is this vice a vice indeed? Is the lie that keeps a man going a cowardly lie? Is a lie all that bad though it is draped over an evil past like a flag over a coffin? False professions and nationalities cover real suffering, and that is enough.

The table of given ages is also doubtful. For the same semesters of February to August 1885 and May to November 1898 I see 197 legionnaires who joined at the age of 18, 146 at 19, 142 at 22, 119 at 23, 118 at 24, 101 at 26, 90 at 27, 76 at 28, 76 at 20, 71 at 25, 45 at 29, 44 at 32, 41 at 30, 36 at 33, 34 at 31, 31 at 34, 25 at 35, 14 at 36, 12 at 38, 11 at 37, 7 at 39, 5 at 40, 3 at 41, 3 at 42, and 1 at 45. Taking this table at face value, let us notice of the median age, for with this figure we see at what age a man is still able to take vigorous action in the face of despair or shame.

But as always, many of the numbers are false, since these men have neither legal status nor birth certificate and are allowed to write whatever they please. One man has seen forty years, but firm on his feet with good vision, he becomes 7 or 8 years younger. Another man is 30 but wishes he was 24 for the sake of a few good stretches of leave-time. Men of 25, 26, 27 or 28 are often not lying overmuch, as this is the normal age. Among those who claim to be from 20 to 23, many are so weakened by misfortune and privation that they claim to be 30, as if they were worn down by age but need only a steady meal to revive themselves, and their lies are accepted. We are left with the legionnaires of 18 or 19 years.

Is this too an illusion?

I was looking over these figures one evening among a circle of officers and I asked aloud if these should be believed, for I doubted them as much as the others. Beside me a decorated captain from

Alsace was also looking over the figures. He had a wide chest bedecked with three rows of medals, a good solid suntanned type who had had to absorb more Vietnamese bullets over the course of his career than there are cherries in a bottle of eau-de-vie. I passed him the paper.

"What do you think, captain," said I, "of these two lines? Do you think these are correct?"

"Nothing that is written on these declarations is true strictly speaking, neither the nationalities nor the ages, and least of all the professions. But there is a method to it all, even in the errors. What do you refer to here exactly?"

"I want to know if these figures are true: 197 legionnaires joined at 18, 146 at 19."

"Yes," said the captain. "Among these 343 legionnaires of 18 to 19 years of age, there are a few who are over 20, but there are many, at least 200, who are only 16."

"And the age limit is 18?"

"We gauge their age by looking at their arms, their lower backs, and their eyes. Then they get their uniforms and that's that. But I've known a lot of men," he said in taking up the paper, "from among these bullshit artists who turn out to be very honorable. Young men of 15 or 16 who swear to be 18 in order to join the Legion. Do you know where most of them come from?"

"No."

"From our annexed provinces. We called them jokingly our *lying children.*"

I set my hand on this sheet of paper and felt a sort of pleasure in it.

"This is their last piece of con artistry," I thought, "and yet there is truth in it."

I saw the pink faces of last evening's detachment and other beardless faces seen by chance among the ranks when the companies began their maneuvers. Men of forty and thirty who lied their way into a future which would leave their old lies in the past. To bring some youthful wholesomeness to these old crooks, lads come up from the mines and down from the pine trees of Alsace and Lorraine bringing along their fresh air. These had but one thing to cover up: Their age. Not only had they entered this world willingly, but they had done so in advance. The Legion says: "You are only a soldier at 18." So they puff out their chests and say in their deepest voice: "Sir, I am eighteen."

If the old lady from the corner store saw such a lad she would shout: "He's lying, he just turned fifteen, just look at the shoulders!" Indeed, these newcomers are just kids, which is why they are precious to the Legion. They complement the presence of all of these aged moral invalids who look upon their youth with perhaps a furtive tear, and certainly they provide a cause to reflect. In the young recruits the old legionnaires catch a whiff of the old life long gone, and more than one of them has been moved by their presence to take stock of his regrets and his squandered life. In a way there is nothing better than the falsehoods I have been examining. After all of the tawdry lies that are spread about once one is in the Legion, the mendacity indulged in upon entering seems to have a certain charm, and the old inhabitants of the barracks must welcome the new *lying children* who will upset the existing order of things for a time.

THE LEGIONNAIRE

I have shown you the manner in which legionnaires first appear. Soon those who have arrived are assimilated into the mass. The Legion is like a terrible sort of hospice which treats impotence with adventure, revolt with devotion, shame with heroism, and despair with death as it gathers in patients and promises them a single cure: Action. Their flesh is offered up to fuel a war machine, to keep the pistons pumping and the gears turning from Tonkin to Madagascar. The gaps are filled and the Legion is made whole, and the *us* which is its source of power will replace the *me* who is the source of its valor.

The passions of all of the various members of a corps combine to form a unit with its own outsized and lively personality, each having its particular virtues, vices, and manias. After a stay at Bel–Abbès and Saïda you can no longer say: "The men of the Foreign Regiments." You must say *Legionnaire.*

At first glance, what distinguishes them from regular French troops is their gaze and their gait. A legionnaire has a glossy or feverish gaze troubled with memories under the invisible rind of forgotten tears. These are the eyes of the dead which still have the power of sight. Their marching pace is jerky.

The instructors oversee a mob of men from the northern nations, the Germans, Belgians, etc, who have learned the drills in their various home nations and are discomfited by the quick pace. They are left to their heavier marching style.

On the road the pace is fast, on the parade ground it is slower.

If you get close enough you can guess at their native lands. Is this one Flemish? This legionnaire hasn't a single spot on his coat, and through a missing button you can see a white undershirt. His flesh is rather white too. He takes good care of his hands and feet and he washes his face energetically as if to wash off an invisible stain. I recall hearing that in the desert colonies south of Oran, if there is no water, a legionnaire will make his own, as it were, if need be…

"We do what must be done."

At the garrison they wash daily and often. If you touch a uniform at any time of the day it is almost always moist. Fifteen minutes after a march they run to a basin and soon the barracks clothesline is full of moist linen. If only there was a washboard for the soul…

When you look into it more closely, you will notice the petty pride of the legionnaire. His uniform

differs from the standard French uniform in that the epaulettes carry a green fringe, and the presence of a wide belt of blue cloth tied around the waist. When out on the town the soldier loosens this belt and allows the scabbard of his bayonet to hang down to the left. He also wears a leather band on his wrist in which can be found his identification card and his registration number. When I was granted a closer look at some of these I could see that many of these leather bands had been inscribed. One night during a concert I saw an etching of a famous woman who looked just as I remembered her.

If you spend time with the legionnaires you come to discover that they know how to do a bit of everything.

In every detachment of the Legion, be it on land or a ship at sea, you can organize a theater group within a matter of minutes.

"Lieutenant, Sir, I played the lead at a theater in Brussels" says one, while a second wrote reviews and a third was a composer.

Two days later a brand new show featuring twenty troops is created complete with a musical score, and the men are entertained as they head off across the Atlantic, or to the south, or to Tonkin.

The other legionnaires do what they can to take up the slack. As soon as the ship is out of port you will find a man assuming the kitchen duty and another working with cargo while a third is tasked with playing cabin boy to some "first class" passenger. This exchange of extra work for a bit of entertainment is defended by most who see the value of it. As for the rest, there are all manner of side-jobs. For a glass of absinthe you will find an able palmist who can read your future from your hand or tell you the contents of an envelope. I was told of a Belgian corporal who taught chemistry to an industrialist bound for Hanoi, and another man who claimed to be Swiss – he painted an Englishman's portrait which now hangs in a London museum! If you throw five francs in among this crowd you will awaken powerful forces, if you throw ten you will give rise to the sublime, and for twenty pure genius will emerge.

How do they speak among themselves? Although they are foreigners, they use our slang, but often improperly. Let me cite an example: A legionnaire from Baden responded to a lieutenant who ordered him to seek out his sergeant-major by saying: *"He is sick of the sea"* (he's seasick), etc...

How do they pass their free time underway? They rarely sing. Perhaps they dream?

There are the mysterious ones, the sad ones, the aloof, the refined, the brutes. Under their uniforms one guesses there may be a soul that weeps. At times their hands tremble, their cheeks go pale, and the memory of a pretty face will make them dreamy or bring in a raft of bad memories.

In the barracks you will find loners called "sitters." Many are willing to converse one on one when moved by some memory or reflection. A man walks past and you hear him speaking of Leibniz, Kant, Wagner, or Pasteur, or perhaps you will hear him tell a dirty joke. Both pearls and filth fall from these mouths which speak in low tones.

You may be sitting next to a simple man who happens to know six languages. Some of them can cite

Latin verses and some Greek. I was shown an Austrian who could write in four slavic languages.

Are they religious?

If a divine figure watches over the Foreign Legion it is without a doubt the Fallen Angel. When a legionnaire dies struck down by a bullet or some fever, a hole is dug within two minutes and filled. But it seems that these men, whose turn it will be soon enough, die too quickly, and one is moved to sadness.

They care nothing for patriotism.

Having run from their nation to our own, they cannot be patriots. But to have chosen the Legion, does it not imply a certain attachment to France? In "marrying" the French nation in such a way that they receive neither advantages nor honors, they undertake our fights. French through alliance, they do not see France as their cradle as most Frenchmen do, but as a bed, which is worth more.

The national sentiment which exalts men of all nations is replaced by their own *esprit de corps.* And the foreign flag they serve and the word *fatherland* is simply replaced by the word *valour.*

The quality of this sentiment will appear mediocre to some. But keep in mind that this word *valour* brought in one thousand eight hundred and forty foreigners in the space of six months, from June to December 1898. 1,840 foreign volunteers of all ages, classes, and intellectual levels who offer up their lives in order to expand our colonies. I always prefer poets to ideologues, and in two lines by the poet Borelli addressed to *the dead soldiers* he reminds the women of France to give a kindly thought to these foreigners, for each man who dies in battle saves the mothers of France the pain of a funeral.

Let us then admire what that word stands for. When the time for departure draws nigh, the officers start the "expedition game." An opinion makes the rounds: *We're headed for Madagascar or to Vietnam, except for the men who are supposed to go to prison, so keep your nose clean, etc.* The majority do not dare to quit the barracks for fear of what a messy bender will buy them. The trick works like a swift kick, and that night the soldiers who do go into town behave like model citizens.

Indeed they are anything but idle soldiers or guys who like to sport around town in a snappy uniform: They want to be where the action is. There was an incident in Paris that you may recall when France's 200th regiment was marching through the city one morning only to disappear, never to be seen again. Instead of rounding them up, they were replaced by legionnaires. These same men of whom their own officers say: "They are terrible when you keep them in the barracks, but whenever the bullets are flying you won't have to go looking for them."

I hang around with them in the street and at the cafes. All they ask is that we send more of them to defend the colonies. We haven't sent nearly enough of them to fight in the south, and yet what have they achieved there? Marvels. If war strengthens their virtues, camp life encourages their vices. These same soldiers that we throw away and try to forget, warriors who will stake their lives, rations, and medals - right up to portions of their heavily tattooed skin - for a single drink, these men are nothing but "placeholders" in a garrison. Of course they cannot live without scandal save under the power of officers who punish rarely, but suddenly and harshly. Such men of action need to move. They become healthy in the open air, and under the burning sun they can support their black memories. They seek only a state of forgetfulness.

That is the man of the Legion as I have observed him. He leaves his blood on the soil of every continent under whatever flag you please. The valour of the regiment comes from the valour of each man, and these men push the limits of the possible. A real exchange will round out this picture:

"Ten men were lost in my company." says a young lieutenant.

"Five." say the older officers.

In any event, the percentage for our regular army is much less flattering.

DEPRESSION

The Legion has one great vice: Alcoholism. There are three major ailments: Malaria, syphilis, and depression.

The first two ailments stem from the climate and the women of the colonies. The third is largely tied to alcoholism, nearly the only vice of a body consisting of some 14,000 men. We shall see that if the vice itself is dangerous, the illness arising from it is much worse.

At the barracks a legionnaire can buy up to ten bottles of wine, and for fifty centimes he can get 10 absinthes. These overly numerous "snacks" (as they are called) could just as easily be called poison, and they are served up by the largely Spanish bar owners who speculate without remorse on ways to squeeze every last miserable cent out of legionnaires. Every drop a man drinks is a year shaved off of his life, and he knows it. And perhaps in knowing it he drinks all the more.

Hardly has he drunk when the booze hits him. His ideas become disordered and his will is sapped as his eyes glaze over. One soldier compares his drunkenness to finally being rid of a little insect which had been gnawing at his brain. That disturbing image has remained with me.

Human beings are possessed of reason, they are not born criminals. The fumes of absinthe will rot the brain just enough for a certain mushroom to grow there, and as it blooms it guards the grey matter from the real enemy: depression.

Hardly has the depression bug been driven away when it returns, crawling across the brain on little legs until it finds a nice fissure to slink into, and there it nests and begins to corrupt all around it. The legionnaire who is gnawed by the bug of despair falls prey to various forms of monomania, fixed ideas which are largely absurd. Certain personal traits make them more susceptible.

One in three men is infected by this malady. He finds himself driven to indulge in risky sex, or acts of revolt, even desertion, and sometimes theft.

When he feels the bug scratching at the inside of his skull and crawling from temple to temple, he will sometimes give his absinthe a pass and head off into the night pretending to go for a drink - only to seek out a certain obliging Spaniard, and make his way to the train station…

Or perhaps he will wander over to the black market and throw his blue sash to an Arab demanding five francs for it. He is offered five sous, which he accepts. Some will buy the sash for 8 cents. In any case a scandal results when in the back streets of Bel-Abbès or Saïda some Spaniard is seen haggling over blue sashes worth six months in prison.

Bayonets are also sold. The brain-bug is so thirsty and the absinthe is so cheap: For 20 cents a man will utterly disarm himself. In return the officer sticks him in a cell.

"You're right, Sir." says the legionnaire, "I should have demanded 15 francs."

Despair is not only for the drinker, it is also for the lover. The brain-bug spins some yarn in a legionnaire's mind which drives him to rape. It puts fire in his eye and causes his mustache to twitch until the demand for perfume becomes unbearable. The bug knows every ruse and trick. I was shown one fellow who had dressed in local garb to infiltrate an Arab tent out of lust.

The brain-bug is also an artist-- a tattoo artist.

I have published a photo showing a legionnaire with a tattoo on his chest featuring a reclining naked woman making a gesture with her hand as if to chase off some overly amorous fantasy she was having. Three little cupid figures fluttered about her, amused at her confusion. This image was entitled *Waking Venus.* I saw another man with a tattoo depicting scenes from a fox hunt on his back. He was adorned with some sixty hunting dogs which spiralled around his legs, bounded down his arms, clambered his up neck, and romped on his chest while armed horsemen escorted a lady's coach. The fox himself could be found in an unmentionable spot, and he was proportioned such that his 'tail' was, so to speak, also the legionnaire's. It was something of a masterpiece.

The brain-bug of despair is deceptive. Just south of Oran two Austrians who hardly knew a word of French were caught abandoning their camp one night. Hardly had they crossed the border when they got nabbed by the gendarmes. In their bags, along with some well forged papers, a dossier full of information on French troop dispositions in Morocco was found. The Austrians explained that the bug had ordered them to travel. Turns out they were former officers with a mind to go home bearing gifts, and even as I write this they are whitewashing the barracks. Although they will never be sent to fight again, they have been given a second chance at life.

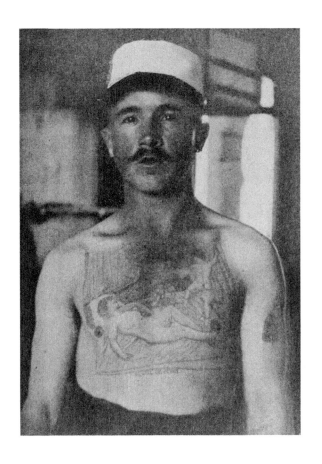

There was an old German in the unit who took leave
of the Legion in France in 1875 only to join the German
army, from which he also took leave. He hitched up with
the Legion again. Then he went back to Prussia, then
returned to the Legion from which he will soon retire. 15
years for France, 15 years for Germany, six years on

leave. French money or German money, honesty here, honesty there, bravery everywhere- what else is there?

Depression leads to forgetfulness. There is a certain old legionnaire from the 2nd Regiment who fought in Mexico among the guerillas, and he cannot remember, when he is asked, whether his company fought for or against the Foreign Legion!

A decorated ex-captain of the marine artillery who had joined the Legion in 1895 was made a corporal (3rd Battalion, 18th Company). He refused to wear his medals from the regular army. He was 35 with a booming voice, and he was big and solid. He could drink three liters of wine at a go. He was a fierce type, and he referred to all spoiled meat as "barbecue." Even when his officers were pleased with his men he would shout: "No, it isn't good enough for my squad!" When he was mad he would not listen to a word. 15 years of service, three in the Legion, he made 700 francs for his retirement and sold his medals for 250 francs. A real character.

Even the protestant minister (it is always a preacher and never a priest who takes such measures) gets the urge to mix things up, such that upon hearing the men speaking a language other than French he asks the colonel to send him all of the illiterate troops. Things go well to begin, with twenty or so legionnaires sitting there by the light of a lamp writing out their letters nice as you please. But then one night the minister arrives late and the students have stolen all of his furniture and have run into town to sell it.

That was the end of school.

A Prussian and a Belgian decided to flee the Legion for Morocco and were AWOL for 8 days. When they returned to the barracks one morning they were disguised as ordinary French soldiers. This story gives those who were there a chuckle every time.

Their journey is worthy of description. Obliged to hide by day and march by night, the two deserters had many empty hours to face. They hatched a plan to improve their wardrobes and return to quarters unharassed in a fine uniform. Some tufts of grass and the hollow of a boulder formed their retreat and their workshop. There, with no other scissors than their bayonets, they transformed their white hats into French "pike-belly" style uniform shirts, while scraps from an old flag furnished their royal blue leggings. Their pants were their own save that they had turned them inside out so that the white piping could not be seen, and these were then cut off at the knees. From the last shreds of their hats they had cut the blue bands in order to furnish the piping for their white culottes which, when tucked into the gaiters, completed the martial illusion. It was only when they stood amid the barracks more or less astonished by the uproar they had created that they abandoned their French soldier act. They were shown to a cell, to which they retired without a word of protest.

The brain-bug sometimes inspires a bizarre kind of heroism. One legionnaire was bringing soup to a man in the stockade only to find the fellow lying there stiff with an empty bowl. He shook the prisoner, set down the full bowl, and went off. The next day another legionnaire came by, called to the man, shook him, pinched him, set down the soup, and brought back the empty bowl. It went on like this for three days. On the one hand the guy was stiff, on the other hand the bowl was empty. A hungry corpse? A doctor was brought in. He entered the cell, spoke, insulted the legionnaire, but nothing happened. Was this a case of catalepsie? Clearly not, since the bowls always came back empty. This legionnaire was goldbricking it.

"Fine!" shouts the major-doctor, "I'll bring back the cauterizing torch and we'll see what's what." The corpse didn't bat an eyelash. The doctor returned. Before beginning, he beat the patient like a quilt full of bedbugs. "I'll burn you good!" said the doctor. *Nothing.* The little flame of the torch touches the skin and there is no movement. The skin is scorched until it sizzles – but then the stockade already stinks. Persistent immobility. The major cooks the legionnaire's heels with no result. Then, furious, he makes a sign to his assistant who goes out and then returns with a bucket. Upon command he throws a bucketful of icy water over the dead man who returns to life immediately shouting: "Ahhhhhh!" This amazingly stoical individual had foreseen every form of torture, but not a bath!

Such incidents are without a doubt provoked by that interplay between alcoholism and despair which gives rise to the bug we Frenchmen often call *le cafard.* I can give you a thousand examples of such lunacy. One morning the captain asks the legionnaire: "You swine, what possible reason can you give for pissing in the mouth of your sleeping sergeant?"

"Captain, Sir!" replies the legionnaire, standing at attention, "I did not wish to soil the barracks!." (True story.)

There was another legionnaire in Vietnam who went to the hospital for malaria, dressed up like a doctor, escaped, went to visit fort Brière de l'Isle, and replied to a rude mail officer by dropping his pants. The reading public will no doubt take comfort in the wisdom of the officers of the Legion who know these men top to bottom and can intervene paternally when they go too far.

But in fact such "crimes" are judged in Oran by officers of the regular French Army who do not know the men, and they judge them as they would some peasant from the provinces. I am in agreement with those who would give *le cafard* itself a seat at such tribunals, to put him on trial or at least make him a witness for the defense. You cannot judge legionnaires unless you have experienced their world.

This institution with a workforce consisting of a 12,000 men should have its own tribunal, a Legionary Counsel of its own composed entirely of legionnaires and their officers. Such a body would hand down sentences that were sometimes more severe and sometimes less so, but they would always be more just. For this reason the French Foreign Legion asks the government of France to undertake a study of new Rules of Discipline.

The first urgent reform, it is widely agreed, would be to reestablish the old bonus system. If a productivity bonus were offered it would keep the men from going into town to sell their sashes and bayonets. Then there would be no need to hold a trial for the theft of five francs, all because *le cafard* was broke.

But nothing is lost. The *cafard* causes so much trouble and holds so much sway over so many minds, and yet we have the means to exterminate him. The general opinion in Bel-Abbès and Saïda is that there is a remedy, and 12,000 legionnaires agree.

There are other less useful ways to be rid of the *le cafard* which are already in use: Fever, bullets, spears, bad air, thirst, hunger, fatigue, and suicide. But let us keep our barracks, that is to say our tiger cages, free of such an infestation.

OFFICERS

In watching officers of the Legion, what is most striking is the number of medals they wear. There are 24 decorated lieutenants in the 2 regiments, all of them owing to valor in combat.

What we notice next is their age range. In France all lieutenants and 2nd lieutenants are from 22 to 35 years old. In the legion I have seen 22 year old 2nd lieutenants working beside 45 and even 50 year old lieutenants.

There is a 47 year old lieutenant here who did his first hitch and left the Legion as a noncom. He rejoined the Legion as a 2nd lieutenant in the reserve during the conquest of Tonkin, and after 2 years in the field he was made a 2nd lieutenant, Regular Legion. This is not the only example. There are many interruptions in service which vary from 5 to 10 years, which serves to explain the variance of age between officers of the Legion and other types of officers.

To see these old-timers side-by-side with youngsters, mixing among them and listening to them, you get the impression that you are indeed among *special forces.*

And of course you are. Whether he comes from the Academy at Saint-Cyr or Saint-Maixent where he was at the top of his class, or he climbed up the ranks through strength of will, or he was regular army and tired of not seeing any action, the Legion officer, upon entering service, undergoes a mysterious transmutation. Facing 12,000 men who watch his every move, the 7 or 8 thousand working brains who take him in, he becomes both elevated and simplified. What was artificial in the officer's bearing falls away, both his restraint and his posturing. Hardly has he arrived among the legionnaires and listened to their talk that he becomes, I will not say more than an officer, but a man of many parts who serves as a judge, a doctor, an administrator, and friend. Such a man becomes, before all else, the master of himself.

Within a few days his life becomes clear to him in its full scope. Though young, the moment he arrives he holds sway over virtue and vice, and he must make the men march in step. To do this he must learn that the regulations are nothing, but necessity grants him other resources.

He goes to the barracks, asks questions, weighs options, and passes judgement as a last resort. He must do this to keep the men under his command from slipping through his fingers. He knows that the strongest chain with which to bind simple souls is the word, and he learns a particular manner of speaking.

He calls the men *tu* (informal you) or *vous* (formal you) with calculation. After some time in the

Legion, the use of these words becomes a veritable art. They bind the good and weigh upon the bad, and even lift men up when they're at rock bottom. The officer says "you" with a whole spectrum of intonations. The single gesture and the proper gaze can increase or decrease the effect. This is not the mechanical *toi* that a regular army officer throws at his men, it is said with great familiarity from a superior friend to an inferior friend. It is not the glacial and indifferent *vous* that every polite Frenchman uses to address an acquaintance or colleague. When an officer of the Legion uses it as a courtesy, "man to man" as it were, with one fellow, it reflects a level of deference that is felt most by those who do not have it, though they might want it, and yet must bear witness.

This cadre of officers, when you have seen them, seem to comprise their own "corps" which is motivated by intelligence, a sense of justice, discipline and courage. I will describe their virtues in that order. The presence of calm in their garrisons shows they are thoughtful men. In this cloistered world which must draw upon its own substance, energy is freed up by order, and this in turn becomes every sort of work that can be done with the hands. Many of these officers have a level of education that exceeds their station.

Commander V… with his big beard, blue eyes, and distinguished nose, once had a Czech soldier under his command in Vietnam that was mysterious, very brave, and a great botanist. The two men made a practice of disregarding French in order to speak to one another in Latin.

"Eo redii, dux, quo certabamus armis heri vesperi, plantamque aliam inveni."

"Ostende... Revers venustissima est. Quomodo nominatur?"

"Gynocardi odorata."

"Diligentissime eam tene... Age vero centurioni dic aliquid esse quod ei praecipere velim in posterum diem. Mane sine dubio pugnandum erit."

Both men had been good students.

But not everyone can speak Latin. Does being less educated mean that one is less intelligent? Not in the least. A wise modesty is worth a vast amount of knowledge. And I know of nothing more admirable than these officers when they gather together in the evening to listen to lectures given to them by a *corporal* who happens to be an ex-colonel from Austria and a genius.

Such men are ready to accept all knowledge, which is to say they pardon appearances. When they do not it is only a matter of maintaining order within the mass of men by holding to severe and general rules. But in isolated cases when they can be sure no reverberations will be felt within the ranks, they apply their very humane and steady good sense. I have already spoken of alcoholism in the Legion. Drunkenness is not dangerous in isolated cases and so is not rigorously punished "as that would have no value."

Take for example the legionnaire who gets shitfaced and spends the night passed out on the edge of the parade grounds. He wakes up and proceeds to piss gallons just at the moment when the officers are coming out for assembly. The man stops his stream and tries to rectify his posture. He offers a salute while stumbling over sideways. The officer salutes him as he hastens to his accustomed spot, and he cannot avoid a grin.

But here is a better example: A captain is bivouacked with with his company. He has just signed an official list containing the names of those he thinks should be considered for promotion to corporal. He hands this list of candidates to the sergeant-major who takes the liberty of adding a few names. The captain finds out and calls in the sergeant-major, saying: "I won't make an issue of this, but you've let me down, and I can't say I will be able to entrust you with much in the future. Dismissed." The sergeant-major walks off. He looks a little pale and goes to the canteen to drink a full quart of anisette. He becomes frantically drunk, grabs a loaded revolver, and runs through camp shouting: "Where's the captain? I've gotta kill him." The captain hears him and comes out. Three men run up to him and say: "The sergeant-major is drunk, Sir. He has a revolver and plans to kill you, and he will if you don't go inside." The captain walks past them and approaches the sergeant-major, saying: "Seems you wish to kill me. Fine, let's go back to your tent. I'll go first to show I'm not scared, and you can shoot me in the back if you're up to it." The two men go off, one following the other. There is terror in the camp. When they enter the tent the captain tells the sergeant-major to set his gun down, which he does. The officer takes the bullets out of the gun and says: "You can't let the men see you in this sorry condition, so go lay down in my tent."

The men tell me that the sergeant-major went to a tribunal the next day, and the story was told. But the sergeant-major had performed bravely in the past, and the captain pardoned him.

On a campaign and under fire drunkenness is treated differently. In a small forward post a man who had drunk too much suddenly breaks the silence. His comrades jump on him to stifle his howls. The lieutenant comes in and the man threatens him. The lieutenant tries to make the man understand that he is putting the whole post in danger, but the legionnaire only yells louder. The officer orders the man to be tied to a bamboo stake beside a pond "where the tiger comes to drink." The shouting redoubles. He is gagged and led off by the lieutenant. The men wait. An hour goes by and the tiger arrives, but the lieutenant is there. He unties the man and without a word he hands him his rifle. The two men kill the tiger, and later the drunk man finds himself up for a promotion to Legionnaire 1st Class.

It is his ability to keep men in line through subtle touches and inquiries that mark out the true officer. He must live among these masses, swimming in them, as it were. And they are almost all Germans! They come from some military or civilian prison harboring one secret vice or another, and yet the officers are indulgent when it comes to such weaknesses. A new officer had better come to know his men better than critics know their books, or he will soon understand that he has made a mistake. But an older officer who becomes too familiar with them is in an even worse state.

Such a case occurred not too long ago. There was a need to even out the troop numbers in various sections. Suddenly a legionnaire standing before the officer saying: "I do not want to change squads."

"Why not?"

"I want to stay with my friend."

"His name?"

The name was given. There was a moment of silence. "So, " said the officer, "do you need to sleep in the same tent as him?"

"Yes, lieutenant."

I asked the storyteller if there were a remedy in such cases.

"Outside of the garrison, yes." he replied, "Out in the colonies where the action is."

The officer did not wish to speak further on the matter.

Regular military men of our day have no understanding of the psychological bond between the legionnaires, and this is largely due to the difference in their time horizons. The regular army is largely for short-term service, whereas the legionnaire's whole existence is bounded by his service time. Thus his day to day life is all about immediate surroundings, and he does not bother to think beyond these. His ambitions are limited by obedience.

We rarely hear talk of the many 2nd lieutenants, lieutenants, and captains, who are all action and silence. Do these taciturn characters suffer in the manner we often hear decried by all of the many humanitarians? It is worse than that, actually. When they read about such protests on their behalf they shudder, as they listen carefully when France is being glorified. But there is no need to raise a ruckus about something when you already love it. They keep quiet with their lips and learn to quiet their brains lest these run contrary to orders. They are mutes who act, the opposite of us Frenchmen.

A gesture made by one of them comes to mind. I was drinking with lieutenant B... who had long been the head of a Legion disciplinary company, when a paper-seller plopped an electoral prospectus on our table.

An outpost in Vietnam.

"Do you guys ever talk politics?" I asked indiscreetly. He was a little shocked, and he leaned over the paper which bore the name of a certain candidate with the title *Final Campaign!*

"Don't know him." he said. With a finger he slid the newspaper off the table.

If you wish to know all of the acts of valor performed by officers of the Legion, pick up the fine book *Historical Deeds* by general Grisot and Roger de Beauvoir, *Camerone* by messieurs L'Aumonier and Saint-Cyr, *Memoir of a Partisan Leader* by commandant Grandin, *Memories and Campaigns* by general de Motterouge, *Generals and Soldiers of Africa* by captain Blanc, *In the land of Steps* by Ecorres, *History of the south Algerian insurrection* by colonel Trumelet, *South of Oran* by captain Armenguard, etc. To the anecdotes found in these works I would add another, one which stays with me. It deals with bravery, a mixture of valor and simplicity which brings to mind the experience of the citizen-soldiers of the Napoleonic Wars.

The gigantic major X… and his wife were accompanied by some legionnaires in a boat on the Tonkin river. It was night. The officer smoked a cigarette and said: "Do you remember, my dear, that article in *Variétés* about the--" At that instant, both shores of the river exploded in gunfire, the bullets whizzing over the water, and one of the soldiers was wounded. "The Annamites." said the big major. He stood up, and when he did so it was as if the boat had a mast. Then, calm as could be, he said with the air of a man ordering coffee: "Seven men to the right, seven to the left. Rowers to your oars. Legionnaires, take a knee and only fire on command. Suzanne, lay down at the bottom of the boat. Left side, take aim, fire! No hurry. Perfect. Don't be afraid Suzanne. Right side, take aim, fire! Darling, get down between the weapons crates there. Right side, aim, fire! Why are you crying dear? We're not in danger. Rowers, brace up. Right side, aim... Hold your fire. Stand down, the Annamites are gone. Anyone wounded? Come on. A hole in the shoulder. Could you grab the medical bag, my dear?" And the giant major sat down, still calm, lit his cigarette, and unrolled his medical kit.

All of these officers are capable of such marvels, and the young ones wait to "take their world tour" so that they can do the same. It is no surprise that such leaders are the masters of their domain. The Legion loves them because it admires them. One officer told me that when the bullets started flying his men would press in around him to keep him safe, to such an extent that he was free to scan the horizon without fear of taking a hit.

Colonel of the 1st brigade

SONGS & COMPLAINTS

A battalion that returned from Ain-Sefra is camped on the plain 25 km from Bel-Abbès. I go to see them. It is their last day under a tent, and they're happy. Everything is being seen too. They have been there for 20 minutes and the tents are all up, the beams are straight, and the animals are being roasted. Each mess kit emits fragrant steam. There is plenty of talk amid the action. There is an argument in German and some Italian curses. Lieutenant S... shows me a man turning over his bit of beef with a fork. "The baron de V..." said he, "Big-time gambler, lost 3 million on roulette. There's Mr. L... who used to be a noncom in the cuirassiers." We converse for a while. The rifles are all stacked and ready. Upon raising my eyes I see a bare chest and head soaked in water. It is the commandant wiping his head with a towel. Then we all notice an enticing aroma. "That's Kirtchner, an Alsatian that the troops call *Sirdar.* Hey, Sirdar, what are you cooking over there?"

"Veal cutlets *à la sauvage."* says he.

"And those are all Bavarians and Prussians." whispers the lieutenant. A blond beside us is reading a novel by Anunzio. You get the impression as you walk around that you are in a miniature Europe that is tumultuous, messy, crowded, and fenced in, then sent off to the borders through some misfortune. We rejoin the commandant who offers us a drink.

"Yes," he says in response to my question, "most of the foreigners are from northern countries."

"Others may be more warlike," says the captain, "but these Germans make the best soldiers."

"Excellent morale."

"Thanks to training."

"So they ask nothing but to march, eh?"

"Yep."

"What makes them so well suited for this?"

"Their past, maybe. It comes back to them, urges them on."

The officer smiles and raises a hand, saying: "It is also that…"

A muted cry of victory comes to our ears and we stand.

The corps of bugles, fifes and drums called *la clique* by the French army and *das Spiel* by the Germans approaches and fills the clear desert sky with their sound. They walk in step spreading an intoxication of sound and rhythm as the drums mark the time. The wild sound of the fife and the blare of the bugle grows and then fades as the procession passes on.

"They really love the fife and drum corps," says one officer, "I mean, it is like a ruckus they are not allowed to raise themselves. Any one of these instruments has an effect, but when they come together in these little parades it is as if they are giving voice to the spirit of the men. Their enthusiasm is their way of asking to be allowed to go and fight. They hear the music with their whole heart. We can almost understand the feeling it evokes in them, but not quite. These men don't live for the next quart of wine, that isn't what they long for. Here they come back again, and you'll hear something different this time."

The *clique* turned and came back toward us. The bugles were raised and the pipes began a melody. It was a familiar tune and I felt a sort of thrill when the lyrics came back to me from long ago like the voice of an old friend. When I was a kid in the Paris suburbs back in the 1870's we used to sing that song. The band approached, beating the drum and playing. It passed right in front of me while the fifes whistled the melody and my brain provided the words.

It was a patriotic tune that defied the Germans, telling them they would no longer own Alsace and Lorraine.

And yet almost all of these legionnaires were Germans! We looked at one another and the officers grinned.

"Who taught them that song?" I asked.

"They like the melody but are unaware of the lyrics. They only knew the words to the marching song of the Legion, the *Blood Sausage*."

A sergeant who overheard us sang the words:

Here we have some blood sausage

Here's some sausage,

Here's some sausage,

For the Alsatians, the Swiss, the men of

Lorraine.

There's none left for the Belgians, etc…

"There are also some German songs they always play, like the *Two Grenadiers* for example, which they love without realizing it is a song in praise of Napoleon (the Napolioum). There are also simpler songs. Lieutenant G… provides you with the song sheets.

<u>1st Couplet</u>

Youck hai! What do I see shining? In the bright rays of the sun? These are the brave Legionnaires! They cross the Rhine. Trou ri alla! We are the merry Legionnaires! Trou ri alla illay! We're merry, yes!

2nd Couplet

The flag is in the midst of our ranks. It flaps merrily in the wind. And we march on. As if it were a parade.

3rd Couplet

The captain leads the way, astride his steady horse. And we the brave Legionnaires, are commanded by his sword.

4th Couplet

When we are in camp, under the light of the moon, we sing for our pleasure, a merry little song. Trou ri alla! Hey! We're merry, yes!

A song that is beloved by all is the one called the *Song of the Pioneers.* It is popular in Germany. Free from the life of the barracks, our men sing it out in the colonies. It reminds them of the garrison, the chow-line, the exercise grounds, the relatively peaceful scenes they would happily return to. In far-flung places like Vietnam and Benin they sing this song with added verve.

There are twenty other songs, some more warlike, with cymbal-clashes to accompany the shouted bits of the refrain, causing one to wince and grimace. They share the same character: The couplets caress the ear with simple sentiments put together in three or so words, then the refrain breaks out like a flock of ferocious birds. When you see the band and listen to them from a distance, you get the impression of children playing, impatient to start some new game, and in they end they wind up playing some mean trick on a stray cat.

But the true "voice" of the Legion is its orchestra. In the Officer's Hall in Bel-Abbès I spent three unforgettable nights listening to everything from Beethoven to Flotow flowing from the strings of violins. My exhausted nerves left me open to the lasting impression of this astonishing music, the clamor of the Legion as a whole, the impersonal plaint of a silent horde given voice through this one channel. Only in this music did I grasp the secret which hangs over the regiments.

I did not know what to expect as the men raised their bows. I no longer recall what song they began with, although it may have been a voluptuous tune by Massenet "for strings alone", but hardly had it begun that it exhaled a passion like the doors of a brick oven when slowly opened, warming my cold face. This was not longer the raucous cry of men who throw themselves into the red smoke of combat. From the dolorous hearts of cellos, the fine-stringed violins, the sobbing throats of flutes, the nervous mouths of coronets and wavering clarinets came a harmonious protest against silence, shame, and dark secrets. It was the bitterness and joy of life's memories, the caress of ancient things, the voice of some god of antiquity, the present, the future, all of the irreparable damage done by human passion given voice through music by twenty men who represented 14,000. In the delirium of these sounds my thoughts flew over all of these transfigured heads, and I understood ineffable joy of being able to give voice to dreams and despair. Here upon the wings of harmony, emotion could ride without fear, without a man having to give voice to it. Like the concept of God, music can be used for anything.

I looked at the faces of the musicians. At first there was a sort of consternation, and then there was a sort of rebirth. The first cello, a Belgian, seemed to wrestle with his instrument. I shall always remember this singular musician- was he ugly, was he handsome? He was both. He was drunk with music and he held his cello to him like a woman. The face of a second violinist flashed majestically at times. His lips moved as if issuing forth a quiet sermon or anathemas...

A brilliant composer named Mr. Salomez led these celebrated violins with ease. My short stay in Bel-Abbès made it impossible for me to hear the true first-chair violinist, however - he was in the stockade. Too bad, since he was said to be incomparable.

This kind of music is precious to the regiment, offering them small doses of a higher world. The strings of the orchestra leave the door of Heaven just slightly ajar. Few people know about these musicians, who must stand aside and cheer for the fife and drum corps as it passes.

An anecdote that suggests the genius of the orchestra states that Saint-Saens himself, who was famous for always being in a hurry, stopped in his tracks while passing through the old port of Oran and asked who was playing. "The Foreign Legion, its orchestra…"

He would have stayed longer, but other dreams beyond the sea forced the composer to board his ship and go. No matter. That moment of hesitation was hommage enough.

ADVENTURERS

The strength of the Legion is the spirit of adventure. Among the regiments you will notice men who are soldiers through a taste for great undertakings. The barracks crush their dreams, and these adventurers fall under two headings: The wholly resigned, and the disappointed.

The resigned are generally simple men who sought action in its outward form, which is to say movement. They are used to running or fighting as a way of life, and they use these abilities under fire or during exercise. They are almost always low ranking. They will come, go, jump, sneer, sing, and fight at the drop of a hat, and this silences their childish inner demon. If they are indifferent to danger, life in the garrison is no problem for them either. They belong to every condition and are content with everything. They are also the sort to desert at any moment.

As you might guess this is not the sort of thing that causes most men to join. There are also men who have fallen victim to some restless dream, the intellectuals of adventure. These comprise a large number of the officers from France.

Among those who stampede toward promises of glory, the majority are from state or military schools. There are foreign officers who come in following some personal debacle, men of high culture and bad conscience, who enroll to rehabilitate their souls. There are those who manage to find a rebirth under fire through patience in this cloister of anonymity, or rather through acts of heroism when deployed to the colonies. Recently there have been many Austrians taking this unique "cure." Then there are the Germans, Russians, Swiss and Belgians. Italian officers only manage to correct themselves partially through this process.

These are the two major types of adventurers: frustrated or intellectual. There are various examples.

Munch, wounded in action in 1893 and thrice decorated, returned to his home in Prussia after five years in the Legion. (Today he serves in the 139th regiment of the Saxon grenadiers). An officer tells me of how he used to correspond with Munch, and the two would write rather meandering and affectionate letters to one another. This officer told me that Munch was ordered by his German superiors to wear his Legion medals at parades and even around town. The Saxon tells of how each time he entered a tavern with his French military medals, the German noncoms present would salute them (not him).

A corporal from the Mexican campaign returned to camp a bit unhinged and was busted down to legionnaire, then promoted back up to corporal. He was then demoted again, and made corporal again. This process was repeated a third time and finally he was simply a legionnaire at last. In 1893 at the age of 55 he was out on the town with the young legionnaires, happy and carefree.

Another fellow left the Legion and returned to Belgium. "I served Leopold." he says sipping his coffee, "I've been to the Indies. Today I serve the French Republic in the Legion." He said this with the oddest smile…

All military medals are worthy of a drink. But when the men drink, they often fall down, and when they fall down it is up to the sergeant to carry them home to the barracks. There they are deposited in a cell. They have made the following contract: The total payout for 3 medals over 3 semesters being 150 francs, the evening they are handed the money they go to the weekly duty officer and leave him 100 francs out of the 150 "with the request to keep their three medals until the party is over." Then they go out and party, drink, and run amok before returning on Sunday morning all shined and polished to claim the second 50 francs. The duty officer gives it to them. The party starts again and they sail on a sea of wine at 2 sous per liter. They are dragged home insensate. Emerging from the cell again, they go back to the duty officer all pale and trembling. The duty officer smiles. What can you do? They are only demanding what is theirs: "Sir! I'm just going out for some wine and female company." Fine. The 50 francs is handed over, and the three legionnaires head out like teenagers whose curfew has been lifted. Hardly have they hit the town when they start downing the absinthe, and then come the arguments and brawls. The next day is the same. The following week you will see them making the devil's bargain, selling their belts for the four hundred blows in the black quarter. With the last of the liquor down they return to the barracks half dead. They sober up in cells, and the following Sunday you will see them twiddling their thumbs while trying to listen to Mozart in the Officer's Hall. But this time there is a difference: They have their medals.

These are the simple ones. With the intelligent ones it is more like this:

An ex-2nd lieutenant of the regular marine infantry joins the Legion, is promoted to corporal, then to sergeant, then secretary to colonel Z… He grows bored filling out the same reports and sending them to brigade headquarters. It is time for the adventurer to free himself. With the great wide open before him he can work miracles, but fence him in and he withers. One day the colonel is "ill". The secretary sneaks into his room, disrobes, puts on the colonel's oversized uniform, buttons it up and straightens it, looks at himself in the mirror, makes some adjustments, then walks out of his office. The men see him and present arms. He walks down the Rue de Mascara and upbraids a young sergeant for leaving his belt-line askew. The sergeant goes off astonished. At night the "colonel" is seen on the town with his pile of gold braid and his uniform hat without the long sun-guard on the back. He tips his hat to working girls and gives one a friendly pinch. She is confused and charmed. He comes across groups of Legionnaires who either flee or salute. He salutes back while holding his riding crop. "Hello, lads, good grub this morning, am I right?"

"Sir, yes sir!"

He wanders the streets for an hour. He gets thirsty and enters a Spanish dance hall where 30 legionnaires stand to salute him before sitting down once more. The proprietor looks a bit uneasy. The colonel is sitting at a table at the back of the cafe to the left. If he was to pay for a round of drinks he's doomed, as he hasn't got a wallet. He orders up a bottle for 25 cents and drinks, though he knows this cheap hooch could blow his cover. After three glasses he flags down a legionnaire and has the guy sit beside him. A half-naked girl is singing up on the stage and he sings along. Two adjutants stand up and examine him. He sinks in his chair and just about gives himself away by muttering "Shit, they're getting wise to me." Yet the "colonel" has five more glasses and begins to shout along with the singer. Several men seize him and a corporal shouts: "That's not the colonel, that's his desk-jockey!"

Four noncoms lead him off to the stockade laughing all the while. They take off his stolen clothes and lay him down as he continues to slur out the words to the song. The real colonel learns what has happened and suddenly he is no longer feeling under the weather.

Another example of an adventurer is L. L…. a 41 year old Napoleon III fanatic and something of a drunkard who joined up in 1877. He became a 2nd lieutenant in 1882, then a commander at Bat' d'Af, and the he re-upped in 1888. He went to Chili in 1889 and served as an infantry lieutenant in the insurgent army from 1890 to 1892. He was wounded in action at Sommo-Santos and made a prisoner of war. He escaped and returned to France. He rejoined the Legion in 1893 in order to have a pension and a tad more glory. I am told that he served in Tonkin with honor and valor. A man who knew him and liked him said: "I had to tell him, as commander of your squad I respect you and that you were once an officer. I won't give you any labor details and I'll only expect you to be there in combat." L. L.... returned to the colonies, became a corporal, got busted down at Bel-Abbès for insubordination, and quit the Legion on the 17th of December 1898. All of that intelligence and energy needed to be applied in some direction.

The same goes for the Marquis de B...., an ex-captain of the artillery who had joined up after some breakdown or other. He was a legionnaire 2nd class in the 2nd regiment in 1894, highly decorated and a heavy drinker. He had a son somewhere who was an excellent officer, and that image did not help the father one bit. When the old man drank too much and he was marched to the stockade, the M.P.s would hear him say: "Agh, if *my lieutenant* could see me now!" To this he would add a respectful and paternal, albeit vague salute.

Finally I will mention a true adventurer, a ball of fire who could never be at ease among the barracks, a wild child who was never able adjust to the daily grind. This is the son of a certain Admiral X... who joined the marine infantry, shot up through the ranks, and was made an officer in the field at Song-Tai in the midst of the flying lead. He resigned from the army upon returning to France to avoid the reforms being put into place at that time. As a sober businessman he would only argue with his family. He felt gagged and muzzled by the humdrum, he was always crackling with excessive energy, and the rat-race was killing him. He sought to calm his nerves by joining the Legion at Saïda as a 2nd class Legionnaire. He was bewildered for the first few days. In the desert everything you touch burns you from the bayonet to the stock, and his heart seemed to be working three times as hard. He decided to hop a train out of the heat, got caught, and was thrown into the stockade for sixty days. During that time, thanks to his prior service and his family connections, he was made a 2nd lieutenant.

A corporal goes to see him. As he enters the prison, the corporal hangs the new lieutenant's medal from a nail on the outside of the door. He enters, announces to the prisoner that he is now an officer, and that the colonel wants to see him. Once he is out of his cell and the corporal shows him his new medal, he is astonished. He wonders if this is somehow part of his punishment.

That same day the new 2nd lieutenant is honored before the regiment with music and flags. From that time a new fire is kindled. He returns to Vietnam and receives a big gash to the face before rotating back to Africa. He has not lost any of his fire. He's like a machine, his nerves and tendons vibrating, his blood always on the boil. He finds fault with everything, abuses the chain of command, breaks it, and finally quits again, still longing for distant lands, for mystery. Finally he undertakes a journey of leisure, vomits up his energetic soul, and comes back to France all domesticated.

We are fools not to use such passion to the profit of the nation. The excesses of such characters almost always have some noble cause behind them, and since the lust for adventure causes them to make trouble, why should we not make use of them? What are their personal faults to us? Besides these arise only from a lack of action. These men require foreign lands, freedom of action, and dangers against which to prove their valor. If the average working-class Frenchman is happy to make himself useful within his homeland and has no interest in expanding our colonies (in large part because he fears disease), let us utilize these impatient men who have tested themselves against fever and fatigue. They make extraordinary pioneers, stabilizing the wild land before calling back to us to come and till the soil.

THE DISILLUSIONED

Right beside the adventurers on the parade ground and the battlefield we find the disillusioned adventurers.

They form a group of passionate individuals, hungry and thirsty for action, always wanting more, never caught off their stride, never satisfied. They tend to become men who harbor silent jealousy or who revolt loudly. These are actually the most sympathetic characters we find among legionnaires.

A rich farmer from Oran loses his fortune at cards and joins the Legion. Will the glory he wins compensate for the money he lost? This drowning soul needs fire to heal him. He sees action, but not the type he was looking for: They make him a cook. Talk about disillusionment.

The corporal who serves as the secretary to the lieutenant in charge of the armory is a deeply tanned man with a pointed beard, an ex-noncom of great learning, excellent in combat, who has deserted six times for six different women. When this Don Juan gets out of the stockade and hits the town, any short skirt makes him gaga. The lovers go off together. They spend time playing house, the spell is broken, he goes back to his cell, gets out, and the process starts all over again. The only lady who has no effect upon this hopeless case is Lady Justice.

Three young officers from Russia flee to the Legion to avoid the consequences of some unknown crime and to find adventure. They discover that the reality is something other than they had imagined, and that the only thing they really could not stand were rules in general. They are from rich families. They grow impatient and remorseful. One day they receive letters from their families and they desert.

Others are lost every day to suicide. There was an Italian who had performed heroically at Adouah only to cut his wrists in a cell with the sharp edge of a medal he earned there because he preferred death to inaction.

Another such is the anarchist Van B... from Holland. His head is high and narrow like a loaf of sugar, he is bald and bearded, and his eyes are quick, dark, and shining. Punished for some crime, he is given hard labor detail. "Work is for a free man," he tells his captain, "and the moment I was sentenced I was no longer free, so I must not work." Refusing an order leads to trial. A nice young officer pleads his insanity case and saves him. He goes back to the barracks full of glee. He is given all of the necessary gear, but it is all second-hand, as this is always the case. The new gear is only ever put into circulation when the old gear is worn out. "Nope!" says the Dutchman, "I was acquitted, meaning that I am innocent, meaning that I am entitled to all new kit." The officer punishes him without anger. The colonel says that since the initial defense was insanity, it was proper to put the man under observation. Retiring to the infirmary, the Dutchman, who is believed by all to be mad, sets up shop, sees to his needs, cares for his body, and generally has a fine time in there. This man who passes for a nut knows enough to say: "I'm entitled to this as a free man, etc." The medics are beside themselves as he yells at them and chases them around, calling them the "Poop Police." Unbalanced by his level-headed delivery, they wind up taking orders from a lunatic. But this all comes to an end. Instead of a looney the man shows himself to be a supreme comedian who is simply tired of life in the barracks. Returning to Bel-Abbès to do his jail-time, he tries the same old tricks to no avail. He does hard time. He will be spending a year in prison making sandals out of cordage, and he will no doubt recall with a smile that he has given thousands of men plenty to laugh about with his "free man" gibberish. I leave it to the reader to decide if he is really guilty.

The need to harness all of these wayward energies and ennoble these passions by presenting them with some goal will be better explained by the story of this old engineer from the Belgian Polytechnic Institute, a tall, gaunt, and haggard man who joined the Legion only to find himself disciplined almost immediately.

He is a shifty-eyed type, his eyes burning like venomous lamps. He takes pleasure in degrading his cellmates. He is the stinking flower of immobility: And yet this worst villain in cell full of rotten legionnaires has cause to complain as well, for he too is a victim of disillusionment.

A melancholy man of 31, long and lean with a blonde mustache and blue eyes, he was waiting to be seen by a much sought-after minister to show him the cannon he had invented which he claimed could smash the most solidly made defenses. After a month of waiting for his meeting the man became frantic. He paced the halls of the ministry and verbally abused the page boys who worked there. Finally the doors opened. He was offered a certain sum which he deemed insufficient. He left without leaving his card and rejoined the Legion at Marseille to return to Bel-Abbès where he was punished for desertion. A colonel learned his story and put him in touch with the relevant authorities, but his new cannon was a no-go. The inventor asked if he could work in the kitchen, and since 1895 this former officer from the German Navy has been doling out the chow to his battalion. Talk about disillusioned!

A lad with a nice face, very small, but intelligent and alert, joins the Legion. The captain of his company questions him, and the soldiers admits to having been one of Italy's elite *Bersagliers* who had "helped the wife of a Florentine prince to go astray." Here is his story:

His comrades-in-arms had made him swear to break off the affair since the husband had gotten wind of it. This stain of dishonor would be upon all *Bersagliers.* The soldier gave his word, but love won out, and he forgot his vow. Placed under arrest by his colonel, he was confined to quarters as he awaited trial. It was only then that he comprehended the pain he had inflicted on his idealistic comrades, so he deserted to the Legion. Once there, a captain began to question him regarding Italian troop movements and so on, to which the Bersaglier replied sadly: "No, no, Captain, sir. It is enough that I have broken one vow." The Frenchman saluted the Italian. But one could see there was something eating at the young man. What did he seek in the Legion? Oblivion in adventure. If there is no adventure one cannot forget. The captain found him in tears, for he had received a letter from his family informing him that a desertion letter had been pasted to the front door of their home. At the end of a year he received a pardon and some money. He deserted, and we are told that he is now doing business in London!

The brother of a rich businessman in Odessa, there is a big, boney, taciturn Pole with a head like a bespectacled Kalmyk who had served 5 years in the Austrian infantry before re-engaging as a cavalryman. He became a noncom before committing some serious infraction. He fled, suffered, stopped for a time in Brussels, sought work, was unable to sustain himself, repented for his sin and prepared for death. Before his second to last last supper he heard that men were wanted for the Panama Canal project. He grabbed his things and took ship, came ashore in the swamps and worked his way up to foreman, got knocked flat by yellow fever, fought it, went through hell, and was at last obliged to go to the dry heat of Africa to nurse his ruined health. Remedies and treatments drained his finances. He quit his cot and got a job breaking rocks for the Biskra-Bathna road. Then he threw aside his hammer and fled to the Trappist Monastery at Staoueli. The monks were moved to pity for this strange, boney-faced man with his sunken eyes and fixed gaze, and they took him in. Without a word this heap of human misery was taken into this tomb of the living. He stayed for six months, the customary time during which the monks will shelter a wandering soul in need of a home. The monks suggested he join the Legion. The man murmured his goodbyes and joined up at Bel-Abbès as a corporal in training at the age of 36. An immediate standout, according the officers - melancholic, silent, but full of energy. He went off to Vietnam and served well in combat. He was made a supply sergeant and returned to Bel-Abbès. Too old, he retired, leaving with praise from colonel Audeoud. Disillusioned and bewildered, he returned to the Trappists who recognized him and gave him some funds to start a business. He renounced adventure, took a wife, and slipped into a life of joyless repose. Here we squandered a resource which could still be serving us very well.

The Viscount de B... hitched up under the name of L... , fought in Vietnam as if he were a gentleman-cadet in the company of his ancestors, returned to Algeria, found himself in a garrison he considers to be too low-class, and so had himself liberated. Some time passes. One day our camp doctor is in Paris and catches a glimpse of a man eating lunch at a fast food establishment on the Rue Saint-Roch, and calls to him. It is the Viscount.

"Hello Doctor, what a joy to see you. How are things?" The doctor learns that the ex-legionnaire was working at a shop selling Chinese art. "It's not Peru," says the Viscount, "But camp life was getting dull. France isn't restless enough."

A son of a member of The Institute, a fun-loving ex-tailor and legionnaire for six months, grew tired of bouncing from one end of the parade ground to the other and between four black lovers and two Spanish whores. He went to the infirmary with a green complexion and pulled up the covers saying: "Major I'm unwell, I've done a lot of shagging. Would you write a letter to my family to send along some Vichy water? My beloved parents will certainly send me some." The major did as he asked, and two weeks later the legionnaire received a case of bottles. Regulation demanded that the officer on watch be present at the opening of the package, and after the crate was opened the officer uncapped a bottle. Between the wire hood and the cork he found a gold Louis. Every bottle had a gold coin, making fifty Louis. The men in the infirmary rejoiced. "You know full well," said the officer to the patient, "that legionnaires can't have money. We'll put this in your savings account."

"Crap." said the legionnaire. "Well, let them hurry up and ship me off to the colonies."

"Behave yourself," replied the lieutenant, "And you'll get your chance."

These men complain because there is no melancholy that can compare to their own, their search for new woes is eternal. They become disillusioned because we pen them up and cannot offer them the total use of their energy, these men who are jealous of martyrs! Several thousand tumultuous souls boiling at Bel-Abbès and Saïda in tight quarters, boilers fit to burst, which will explode of their own accord from time to time if we don't open the pressure valve. And so I return to my former point of giving them what they crave, to let them get new air in their lungs, to hurl this energetic mass of men into action! Otherwise you will have a den of vices. And vices can be pardoned when, as in this case, they are the byproducts of virtue.

THE MYSTERIOUS ONES

I now come to the most dramatic sort of men to be found in the Legion. These are the secretive souls, the mysterious ones.

Unconscious gestures of universal action, misunderstanding projected upon the unknown, we human beings are all living mysteries, but we possess certain qualities by which we are defined, if not known. The men I speak of here have suppressed even these. The more civil they are, the more colorful their past. They show up one fine morning and sign on with the Legion which grants them a name, clothing, food, and marching orders. These are newborns who are fully grown, and often they come from hell.

They tend to have the most attractive faces. They have murderous features deformed superbly by woe. You want to give some tragic reason for these red-rimmed eyes, eyes which burn behind a screen, these sunburnt brows, these expressive lips thick or thin, these outbursts and spasms, these attitudes of hatred, regret or despair, and you cannot, because they don't want you to. They don't want anyone to say anything about what they have done in the life they left behind. Headstrong and respectful, cold and grave, they watch their new officers with an attitude which signifies: "I await your commands, be happy with my brief responses. My name is my serial number, and I was born yesterday. I'm one day old."

They enter the squad, they learn the drills, they come and go, march, gallop, and speak of whatever you please, except themselves. And finally they are made to kill: That is all you need to know and all you will ever know. But at the bottom of this mystery you can guess at a considerable passion. I sought to translate the meaning of even their vaguest gestures and tics. The tone of voice, the lines of the face, all of these are facts. I offer these shreds to the reader so that he can weave his own story. Perhaps someone other than myself can push past these doors into their darkness.

A certain lieutenant told me one evening that he had known a man in the Legion with a majestic bearing. He was solid and his gaze was haunted in some way. He had read everything and he understood everything, he was immensely brave, and he never said a word about his past. Whenever he performed under fire he was offered a promotion, and he refused each time. The lieutenant tells me: "Had he wanted to, the man would be a colonel by now."

Another young man joined up in 1893. He was an energetic soldier, quite uninhibited. He left for Vietnam without a word, did his duty quietly, and returned to Bel-Abbès, then left in 1898. His officers learned by accident that he had been "first tenor at the Theater de la Monnaie in Brussels." This nightingale had sought a change of climate, and since no one was the wiser, he had remained silent for 5 years. Where was he singing now, and how?

One legionnaire who claimed to be a Belgian professor of mathematics entered his squad and performed every drill perfectly. They put him in with some corporals in training and he performed flawlessly. One had they impression that he was not learning, he was merely starting over. He told his lieutenant: "I have a good memory and I have just read all of the instruction manuals. I ask to be exempted from these courses." The lieutenant tested him and found him to be more "squared away" than any instructor-captain. He was exempted. Some time afterward a general came to review the troops at Bel-Abbès. He stopped before this man and looked hard at him... After an awkward silence he shook the man's hand and continued on with his inspection. Struck by this scene, Lieutenant B... went to the ledger and gazed at the name for a time, moved some of the letters around, and came up with a new French name. Guided by instinct he consulted the register from Saint-Cyr. Then he went among the ranks and said to the soldier: "You're name is Mr. X... and you're a lieutenant. Let me shake your hand as well." The legionnaire lowered his head and thrust out his hand, which was no longer an officer's hand but a leathery claw hardened by the shovel and the pick. Then everything sunk back into mystery, both the most discreet officer and the most ashamed soldier.

There was a tall German with blue eyes who joined in 1892 under the name of Count de Bandissen, and this man never gave anything away. His life in his chamber was silent and cold, almost invisible, monkish. He left for Vietnam in 1894, was in every battle, marched into fire, very brave, very calm, heavy, simple --very German. He would daydream amid the flying bullets while smoking his pipe like a bear in a swarm of bees. A bullet severed an artery in his leg. He was taken to Cho-Ra. "My time is up," said he, "Just leave it." He asked for his pipe, and he bled to death. Four months later a letter arrived at Cho-Ra asking if Bandissen had left anything behind. The captain was informed, and he learned that the brave soldier was an ex-German officer, the Count of Bandissen, son of the old governor-general of Magdebourg. As for the why and wherefore, it was all a mystery…

22 years old, beardless, tawny as old ivory in a museum, a resolute face until animated, soft and slack in the ranks. He meets with a jolly sergeant while carrying his chow bowl: "Come here, legionnaire!" The man approaches. The noncom says in a low voice: "Don't you recognize me?"

"No."

"But we used to party together at Maxim's."

"You are in error, Sir."

"Well then, maybe you should take the trip to Vietnam if you don't want anyone to know who you are. In fact I too buried my old self when I came to the Legion. Dismissed."

And the two high society gentlemen parted ways.

A former Spanish naval officer got himself discharged and resumed voluntary service during the Greco-Turkish war, and later stopped over in Nice where he his ability to speak French caused him to stand out. He played up the part of the savvy foreigner in order to gamble with the high rollers, lost everything, and proceeded to accuse all Frenchmen of being cheaters. He calmed down and hovered between the Legion and suicide. The regiment welcomed him in. The ranks of corporals-in-training seemed to heal him. Good conduct, but defiant. One day he fell ill. An officer questioned him, discovered his real name and an address, and wrote to his family. The legionnaire's aunt sent the following response:

First, thank you for your kindness to my nephew. The poor boy has already done so many stupid things and made so many vain promises, that I could in no way guarantee that he would return to your regiment once his medical leave was at an end. At home he would find too many temptations, and the border would be too tempting for him. His suffering has been too short thus far, and it is with real pain that I must refuse him my hospitality.

At the same time a cousin of the deathly ill man sent this dispatch:

Make arrangements for his body and soul.

This inflexible letter was the final result of old and unforgivable shame. I asked for further information, but the officers remained silent. They knew the mystery and respected it.

Here is another letter from a French officer to one of his colleagues in the Legion:

You have in your company my nephew who, at the age of 32, just signed up for a five year hitch in the 1st Legion. Why? I don't know. Some girl no doubt, etc.

A terrible story perhaps.

I would be forgetting the best example if I were to leave out this curious page by a remarkable writer named Paul Ginisty. The following excerpt from *The*

Little Marseillais written in January of 1893 shows the public, powerfully, the many mysterious resources of these regiments:

General Castagny had just finished subduing several small Mexican towns. The terrified inhabitants refused to sell their goods to our troops.

"Sirs," said the general to his chiefs-of-staff, "It is expedient to modify the impression that we have produced. This town is very religious. They will have a better opinion of us if we show our respect for the faith. Tomorrow, therefore, we will attend mass and show great solemnity wearing our dress uniforms."

And indeed the next day the soldiers arrived at the church in such a way as to lend the mass as much dignity as possible. They brought forth flowers and palms with which to adorn the altar. Drummers and buglers stood in the nave to lend pomp to opening procession. But the parish priest had disappeared... They looked up and down but they could not find him. No doubt he feared mistreatment.

What to do? They knocked at the door of a neighboring convent. The monks had barricaded themselves inside and would give no answer. For the general it became a point of pride- the mass must go on. And yet there was no one left to perform the ceremony, until a sentry at the door of the church came forward, saluted, and said with respect:

"General, Sir. If you can't find anyone I can say the mass myself. I know it by heart."

"You?"

"Indeed sir," responded the legionnaire, "Before joining up I was a bishop."

Naturally the General stood there astonished for a moment. Then, reflecting upon his resolution, he said:

"Well then, so be it!"

The legionnaire gave his rifle to a comrade, donned his cassock in the sacristy and, assisted by a lieutenant who served as his altar boy, he celebrated the mass with perfect dignity. During the general exordc, after the offertory, the soldier asked if he ought to give a homily. The general decided against it. But when the legionnaire had taken off his priestly robes, he was thanked profusely.

The desired effect was produced. The populace was reassured, seeing that Frenchmen weren't a pack of devils, since they went to mass. The former bishop went on to fight and to fight well, for in the course of the campaign he received the military medal.

Now this one is a real enigma: Albrecht Friederick, son of Friederick and Friedericka Nornemann, born October 15, 1871, joined the 2nd Legion in 1897. This man of 26, sleepy and serious, could he possibly endure the first months of training? He showed up one evening, said only his name and that of his mother and father, and then fell silent and looked sad. He had long fine hands and he saluted properly. But he later became friendly and smiled, sitting among his new comrades and listening to their stories and telling his own, speaking words which were strangely resonant, as if old crystal had been tapped. Then his smile is gone and he becomes dreamy until the night comes down. He knows his drills but his rifle is heavy. Long and slim, he rolls himself up in the covers of his modest iron cot like a greyhound belonging to some king as it drowses on a rug somewhere in the palace. What can be the cause of the tear which forms at the corner of his eye as he lays there unseeing, bored or amused by thoughts of a world long dead to him? He falls into a wretched state and command terminates his engagement. He is sent off to a military hospital after only ten months in the Legion. Too late. He dies while waiting to be sent on medical leave, quietly as ever. To the astonishment of all, a ship arrives in the harbor three days later to claim his body. It is an ambassador who, on the 27th of November, comes to ask for the remains of "Albert Friederick." He is the first cousin to Henry of Prussia, thus the cousin of Wilhelm II, Emperor of Germany. And the great ship decked with black bunting sails off back to Hamburg.

Why do I add such anecdotes?

I seek only to inspire reflection in the reader. Let him search his memory for those dark moments when he considers quitting the world, perhaps to find new hopes and a new soul. These men are born of such moments. They carry the memory of a first life into the silence of a second. Of the first life we know nothing, nor shall we ever. Mysteries and darkness... If we were to put our ears to their hearts in the manner of an American Indian who puts his ear to the earth to listen for distant rumors, we shall no doubt hear whispers of the old life, the first life, in which some ancient drama lies hidden. There are defeats and triumphs, calls for help. Shattered illusions, muted cries, financial disasters, sobs of love, cries, moans, and here and there, like bubbles rising from muddy water, we hear the occasional gunshot...

REFORM

I have tried to show the visible part of the souls of these men, and I stop short of the darkness. I am curious to find the truly magnificent shipwrecks of the soul, but in looking too hard I am likely to find rather vile detritus. Thus I stop short. I hang the heavy lantern at the mouth of the cavern. What could be down there? Vice, virtue, splendor, disaster, dried roses or animated corpses? No one can be sure. Thus let us not descend, but remain at the doorstep and ponder the mystery.

Then we return to the surface, for above this silence there is a turbulent crowd. Down below, dark and heavy smoke, and up above, light, life, and vibration. As the roots strike downward new power rises toward the sky: The Foreign Legion is like a tree. It is a massive tree nourished by the contents of a hidden tomb. The branches strike outward to the colonies giving the shade of 14,000 leaves. But there is a worm gnawing at the tree.

I did not go looking for the little critter, it was shown to me. The Legion seeks to transform its recruitment and training strategy.

When a legionnaire joins up from no matter where in France, he has to go through his local mayor. If he seems robust enough they let him sign up. What happens with foreigners? I leave it to a legionnaire to explain. He works at the press office at Bel-Abbès, a tall young foreigner, an artist with pale hair and eyes like a watercolor. Jeremiah shows me his illustrated memoirs: These are full of sketches which are miraculously accurate. In the first two pages we read:

The destiny of man is curious, above all in the case of one who, for whatever reason, be it misfortune or poverty, has been cast out of paradise and falls into a life of adventure.

My friends, I had a talent for painting and a good position in a great artist's workshop, and my parents wished me all of the best. But in my young brain certain ideas, or rather dreams, began to take up more and more space, and one fine day, led on by the splendid weather of May and wishing to see foreign lands, I took leave of my native land and headed for Switzerland. Being young, I took no thought for the morrow. I passed over Saint-Gothard where I admired the wondrous landscapes but, upon entering Italy, I found that my slim funds were already exhausted. I came to know poverty as there was no work to be found. I went three days without eating. I was obliged to go to the police station to avoid sleeping out in the open, and I was exhausted after having walked 75 kilometers. They *housed me in a little dark and airless cell fit for an animal. During that time I heard much talk of the Legion. To keep a long story short I entered France and joined up at a garrison near the town of Mâcon (Haute-Saône) near Lyon.*

There I filled out my papers and was examined by a doctor with two stripes who found me healthy, robust, and of sound constitution. They gave me my marching orders and 2 francs fifty for the two days I would have to lodge in Marseille. I returned to the town of Mâcon at 8:00 pm.

Jeremiah took the train, arrived in Marseille, and walked around. He looked at the sea, the sailboats, and the dirty streets (blamed on the Italians residing there), as he made his way to Fort Saint-Jean. He gave his papers to the post commander and was led before the executive officer's desk. From there he climbed a staircase and joined the men.

Finally I arrived at the platform where I found the men of the Algerian regiments, fresh recruits, and other troops from Africa who were on leave or had been discharged.

There were all types there wearing all manner of civilian garb, and each had his reason for coming here to hitch up. There were some who were simply impoverished, some with family troubles, some who had had bad love affairs, and some who had screwed up with the Law and had to flee. Among these last were some bad characters, though they were young, and did not know what they were doing.

There were men from all branches of the Legion in their various wild uniforms, from the Zouaves with their huge leggings, to the tirailleurs, the chasseurs, and the spahis.

From the platform we had an excellent view of the city. Before us along the quai there was a beautiful church, the Gloriette, done in the Byzantine style...

I was in the midst of contemplating the horizon when a man stuck a mop in my hand and commanded me in a terrible voice to clean the latrines. I began to have serious misgivings about the Legion since I had the mop in my hand until noon, when it was time to go eat a lunch of not-too-greasy baked beans, a little slab of meat and a handful of bread…

It was out on the immensity of the ocean that memories of the homeland and the good old days assailed the mind of this poor traveller…

I raised my eyes, and in the distance I could discern the land where I would live a life of adventure, I told myself, as a soldier of the Foreign Legion.

There was no other form of surveillance or formality from the time he signed up to the time he arrived in Marseille. For all of that time Jeremiah was on his own. He is honest, he had given his word. But what is to stop a scammer from selling his marching orders and his train ticket to some malingerer?

Unfortunately there are many such men in the Legion. These are people who are weakened by prolonged privation and misfortune, a mass of sunken-chested wretches who make unimaginable efforts to slip into the ranks of the Legion. But once their boots are on the ground and there is nothing left to give but heroism, these apparent weaklings often prove the strongest, for true vigor comes from the soul.

But you cannot count on heroism alone, as combat is not an everyday affair. The colonies demand soldiers with solid muscles and good lungs. For this reason the Legion is asking that a Physical Assessment Office be established in Marseille. After a man joins up and his papers are sent to the regiment, he must be verified by a doctor.

As for personnel management, there are only two bases at Bel-Abbès and a little base at Oran to receive all of the incoming recruits while sending off troops on leave and discharged legionnaires to France.

The two companies at the Bel-Abbès base have a force of 800, 1,000, or sometimes 1,200 men, whereas active companies have 250 or 200.

The groups of 800 to 1,200 men are commanded by a single captain, a single lieutenant, and the same number of noncoms and corporals as an ordinary company.

If the new recruits arrive together, a strong hand can guide them, but they come in dribs and drabs of 20 to 30 men. Each group requires a drill instructor, and since they come in ceaselessly the instructors get exhausted. If the captain and the lieutenant, after having lodged, armed, dressed, and fed the men wish to administer justice as well, what will they have left for the education of their legionnaires, especially in a matter as complex as marksmanship?

Currently a lack of noncoms forces the captain to designate random soldiers as squad leaders, the heads of training groups, and the masters of sleeping quarters. It is well known that every time a man is vested with an authority he does not deserve he begins to abuse it.

What follows is disorder. At the end of several days voices cry out for justice. The ad hoc leaders of low or mediocre character who are tasked with directing all of this energy find themselves at the head of grumbling squads or even an angry mob which can only be moved when menaced by the Regulations. If an officer should come upon them and see the sorry state of things he may move to set things straight, appease various hatreds, and lift some spirits. But often he does not come upon them, as he has no time.

Another danger is that at these bases a large number of old legionnaires who have done a number of tours now work at various jobs around camp (gardener, muleskinner, shoemaker, tailor, shopkeeper, etc.) They have come from the colonies to convalesce. Often they are men who have seen and done it all, and here they are mixed in with a mass of youths from 16 to perhaps 18 who have just arrived – at times this can lead to serious ugliness. In the presence of these jaded veterans who often reside in cells, the young recruits become demoralized. Exploited by the old-timers they can in turn become loose cannons, taking on terrible habits. Drunkenness tops the list, with recruits going off on six day absinthe benders only to get sent to the stockade. But if you were to seek out the root cause of this debauchery you would have to look to the misbehavior of the veterans.

One proof that this whole system is defective is that once these recruits are sent to active units, the same legionnaires behave perfectly. They now obey every command from sergeants, officers, and corporals, and the whole company falls in line behind the captain. One man can look after the whole group.

The reform that needs to be instituted simply consists in adding more drill instructors to the bases at Saïda and Bel-Abbès. Then we will not see a single 2nd lieutenant in charge of 800 to 1,200 men – and what men!

While this lack is being supplied on a permanent basis the Legion can send every available and reputable sergeant and corporal who may be convalescing in the colonies to fill the gap. The men will be better and more quickly instructed and the contagion of immorality and revolt will be contained.

If I had to choose between the Physical Assessment Office at Marseille and the additional drill instructors at these two bases, I would say the latter takes precedence.

Next the Legion should form a special corps for the youths of Alsace and Lorraine who arrive very young and very innocent, honest, and upright. They have no faults to hide, no memory to bury, and no murders to flee from. These lads are thrown at random into a mob with a few saints and many bandits, and if they take a bad turn we have only ourselves to blame. Despite diplomatic scruples we should form an Alsace Lorraine battalion, at which point enrollment will double.

What about Poland? And what of poor holy Ireland so often beaten and betrayed? Ireland which our brave Humbert defended against the English in 1798, Ireland where being French constitutes the best passport from one end of the green island to the other? Poor deserted and desolated Erin who loves us and has believed in us for 50 years and more, what a formidable battalion she would furnish for

France, if only France ceased to treat her as a stranger!

With these four battalions: Alsace, Lorraine, Ireland, and Poland, we could create a 3rd Regiment for the Foreign Legion.

TWO COLONIAL ARMIES

All along the Chinese frontier, the line of little posts called "Mixed Border Police Posts" are manned by Vietnamese troops. It is an economical system for France. We furnish them with a bit of rice and these expert bushwhackers make top-notch guides, though their utility ends there.

Forgetting that the needs of Europeans are more costly and that their requirements while on expedition call for more expensive provisions, and considering only the service they can render us, we would have in these men the kernel of a powerful future colonial army.

We shall of course have to place tireless French officers at the head of any Indo-Chinese units, for as it stands these men cannot stand up to the kind of fire almost any European unit would offer. The Vietnamese are brave, but they currently lack an offensive drive and the necessary physical endurance. Troops from Senegal, Sudan, and Arabia are like colossi next to the Vietnamese, sometimes to a nearly superhuman degree. If during an action in Vietnam our own troops do not appear to sustain the charge, the indigenous troops are immediately put to route. Europeans remain the best soldiers for the colonies.

Muscularity and morale have to be developed. The training hubs of Bel-Abbès and Saïda are well adapted to offering this service. We ought to have

Vietnamese troops sign on for five years, and many will rejoin three times running. They cost less for the state because they are offered neither joining bonus nor a rejoining bonus, and they are numerous since the doors to the Legion are always open and men flow into it ceaselessly. There is another reason for making these units the core of a great army of adventure, and this is that the legionnaire himself, a being of rough temperament and audacious soul, is so to speak 'vaccinated' by a bitter life against the hardships to come, be it fire or disease.

As for the rest, once he joins it is his sole desire to travel the world, to hurl himself onto the shores of far-off seas or creep through some swamp. "The légionnaire is an outlaw." said colonel de Villebois-Mareuil, who had himself leapt over the boundary of a society where he felt ill at ease thirsting after mortal danger, to risk his life, the only thing he had to wager and with which he gambled well. "If emulation and circumstances develop an admirable spirit in him, he responds to the monotony of the barracks through a disdainful indifference to the perfection of drills, a willfulness in not doing a whit more than he must, and the frank sentiment that one does not become a soldier to give a damn about peace-time concerns."

And yet far from setting him loose, France pens him in with his demons, leaving him to fall back on his memories.

It seems to me that we ought to make use of all of this magnificent energy. What good are these reserves who do not march, or march too little? Among a total of 14,000 legionnaires we could form colonial battalions from men who have been on campaign. Intelligent, brave, adroit, expert in many fields— such men would form a "Colonial Guard" which could accomplish miracles!

This is a colonial army as many Frenchmen would like to see it. I hope this will develop into more than some side-project. But here it runs into another formidable organization which clutches its prey like a vulture: the National Colonial Army.

Three days before their departure for Tananarive, the men of an outgoing battalion formed groups on the terraces of the cabarets in the town of Bel-Abbès as night came down. I was drawn to a table where I found intelligent men: former notaries, lawyers, doctors, writers, engineers, monks, and artists were gathered. Other tables were full of men whispering furtively, but at this table the men spoke loud. They had been on expedition, and they were wearing medals. I sat among them as they spoke of the colonies, the administration, and civil servants.

As I listened I jotted notes at random, taking down whatever I could hear clearly. I will let the men speak to the reader:

In the colonies all of the Frenchmen you meet are civil servants.

In 1887 there were 600 Europeans in Hanoi, 500 of which were civil servants.

In Ténès there were a dozen Frenchmen, all high-level civil servants. On the other hand the Spaniards, Germans, Belgians, Italians, etc - were all working men. I knew a Maltese businessman who got very rich.

In Son-Tay in 1886 there was a man, a chancellor in residence, and six employees to minister to just three Europeans, the most "honorable" of which was a spice-merchant, a Frenchman who was under surveillance by our federal police.

In 1895 when we were heading off on an expedition in April, 2 station chiefs and 125 judges were leaving at the same time as the soldiers. At the present time (1898) there wasn't but 100 meters of railroad, and I cannot imagine what there was for 125 judges to judge in Madagascar.

The French love civil service - or civil servants - so much that under the pretext of attracting hardworking mandarins they gave them a fixed salary. We appoint them now!

Oh, the civil service! An assassin in Conakry was condemned to death. He was a dangerous man who was going to be made an example of. Since there was no guillotine, he stayed in prison eating better than any soldier.

"I could shoot him." said a captain of the Legion.

"No," said the governor, "The law demands that he be guillotined."

"Morality, or rather the common interest, calls for his death." said the captain, who was allowed to speak freely. "Two legionnaires will send him to the devil, since there's no guillotine here."

"What about the newspapers?" murmured the governor.

The newspapers were a problem of course, but what the civil servant feared most were the three or four other European colonial agents, one of whom was a German whose very presence caused him to watch his every move.

"In the same sized territory the Brits will have one man, while we will send fifteen."

Etc, etc…

And the men speaking had seen all of this.

Here we have two armies side by side, one of which receives nothing from our country and yet gives its life. By contrast the other army is inept, while receiving from France honor and fortune which only makes it lazier.

Let the legionnaires laugh when they have to present arms to these clowns! If the governor-general were to take the rifle from one of these soldiers and promote him to a position of power, within a month we would find a colony that was lean, happy, and efficient, administered by the men that no one believed in. Resolute, knowledgeable, energetic, these are soldiers who are paid ten cents on the dollar!

This is a joke, but there is truth in jest. I joke to highlight the fact that the state sends our superfluous men to the colonies, the dimwit sons of families elevated by marriage, numbskulls and good-for-nothings, some so delicate that it would seem someone forgot to bury them. Then mama says: "Son of mine, since you don't want to do anything, I found you this excellent post…" But what happens to these feeble hearts and rubber spines under the scorching sun? The Legion knows well.

At the same time the real men of the colonial army are thinking: "When I reach retirement they'll send me off, and yet I'd be better off here with a post. But such posts are reserved for the young dandies with nothing to do in France. I guess I'll head to Paris. There I will be with masses of old legionnaires, and I shall have to stand in line for a retirement job. I'll stuff my medals away and hang around the banks of the Seine smoking my pipe, since that is all I'll be able to afford to do."

There are a vast number of down and out legionnaires wandering around in Paris, some sleeping under bridges. Brave soldiers who loyally served a nation for four sous a day, or eight under fire. When their service is done we forget them and toss them aside – and yet it would be so easy to save them!

We could simply offer them administrative posts in the colonies. Among these men of wide understanding we would find all of the necessary qualities for agents of every sort, postmen, industrialists, vintners, men who are used to working out under the sky, happy to begin a new existence far from the towns without drama and incident. What spirit they would be imbued with when offered a chance at deliverance! After campaigning in the colonies with fire and sword they will work with the pen or the plow. There is still so much to be done in Madagascar, Vietnam, and Sudan. There is law to be upheld and order to be imposed.

I conclude by asking that a Colonial Army composed of these heroic regiments be added to the Legion, and posts in the colonies be filled by old legionnaires found to be honorable, healthy, and energetic. Squandered energy tortures a legionnaire. I have just written a book about them and conclusions all point toward the same thing. The leitmotiv of my study has been *to make use of the Legionnaire, to employ him ceaselessly, in no matter what fashion, in battle and in the garden, for everywhere he shall show his worth!* Indeed, if the combat value of such men be well known, their peacetime virtues are ignored. When one of their battalions is dug in out on the vast desert of the Bled among the dunes and the dust, just watch them tranquilly raising their tents. Within an hour there will be water, by nightfall a well, on the next day a field is marked out, and at the end of 8 days seeds are sprouting. In two weeks there are houses and in six months there is a town which the troops can govern just as they built it. There you will find judges, architects, engineers, scribes to start a newspaper, accountants to manage a bank, industrialists to open a factory, farmers to work the fields, and even noblemen to conduct smooth relations. This mass of men made honest after the faults they have committed through time spent in the martial cloister, through the prayer of energy or the

High Mass of cannon-fire, these civilizers who can make miracles, these men are currently languishing without direction. Let us act quickly to save them.

TO MADAGASCAR

I had just finished tidying up my notes. I was ready to leave Bel-Abbès when an officer informed me that a detachment of the Legion was ready to leave for Madagascar.

To go with them at a moment's notice would serve to round out my observations "in the field." I had tried, in my notes, to capture the life of the regiments, not through psychological description, but through a description of their own responses. But to get out there under fire – would that not be the ultimate means of understanding them? The next morning I was at the gate.

Departure was at 7:00 am.

The detachment headed for the station to the sound of the fife and drum. Here comes colonel Bertrand in his Kepi, and here stands captain Delavau who commands the detachment. To the right are lieutenants Colombat and Taste: Here are the Legions ready to fight for us.

There are 135 of them led by 8 corporals. On each chest there are colonial medals gleaming, and 100 men out of 135 have one or two wounded in combat medals.

You can discern their nationalities. There are many Germans and among these many Prussians. There are many golden beards, Italians with deep black eyes, olive skinned Spaniards, solid Flemish skulls.

There is a passion in their eyes. Some are insolent like a crime committed at noon, some are morose, some look lost, and yet this is why they are here, audacious, haunted by memories, proud and unseeing. Youths who dream of glory, rascals running from vice.

Their pace shows their spirit, they all seem to hasten toward the vision which calls to them: Madagascar, far away, calls with open arms. For some it will mean a good death, for others forgetfulness, for most just adventure, and for the officers it means the glory of a greater France.

Departure from Bel-Abbès. The music blares on the railroad platform. The sky is overcast. Captain Delavau holds a wreath sent by the Lady's Society of France. The officers who are staying are envious of those who are going. They say their goodbyes with energy.

"Embark!"

The men mount the train in silence. There is not a shout, no one speaks. With the men aboard the lieutenants climb up. The train whistles. On the platform with their heels squared and their right arms just so the 1st Legion salutes. The train departs. Then the colonel lets his arm drop. The conductor lowers his baton and the music stops all at once.

At Oran the detachment takes up their bags and marches through the familiar town. The Legionnaires of Bel-Abbès are joined by those of Saïda. There are 95 white helmets, two sabers belonging to captains Lamarque and Toury, then three lieutenants. Handshakes and a few words: "We're campaigning together." "Great." "We might see Machin and Chose over there." "Machin's dead."

"Poor bastard." "What should we drink?" I take a seat and witness a short drama in three parts.

A legionnaire from the 1st Regiment, a man of 25 who looks sturdy and strong, decorated with the Legion of Honor, is approached by a young lieutenant from the 2nd Regiment. This other fellow has a big beard with a long mustache, and he stops short with his head held high four paces from his superior officer. The officer recognizes him and blanches a bit.

"Lieutenant." says the soldier, "I just learned that you are part of the detachment headed to Madagascar, and as I am going as well, I thought it my duty to present myself to you."

The officer says:

"Quite right, thank you."

There is an uncomfortable silence, and then:

"I know," says the soldier, "that I have a lot to make up for."

"Yes, a lot…" says the young lieutenant, "So we will see what you can do over there."

They salute and the legionnaire goes off.

"Who is that?" I ask.

"That's one of our old comrades from the 2nd. He was a lieutenant twice, twice demoted for lack of dignity in service. He rejoined as a Legionnaire 2nd class. He's a drunk when he hangs around the barracks, an opium smoker, he even sniffs ether – he did all of that over in the colonies. It happens to the best. They see a lot of action and when it's done they get crazy. He was an officer just like us, we were tight, and I respected him as a hero. Just now when I saw him I forgot all of the rest and I was about to salute him."

"And the medal?"

"He got it at Lang-co-Loun in Vietnam. He was wounded. But if I were in his shoes I would only wear it in the field."

We watched him walk off, and it was a sad moment…

On Tuesday night all of the men are arranged along the quai facing the ship. General de Ganay, an old African, is escorted by general Maudit, an old lieutenant-colonel of the Legion who was at Tonkin and Dahmoney. They are reviewing the detachments.

Sometimes the general will stop among the men, touch a chest full of medals, and smile.

Among the merchant stalls stand a thousand spectators, duly impressed. Are they seen as saints or assassins by the crowd? Anxious women emerge from the mob. The breeze plays over the sea carrying the music of the Zouaves, a single sob is heard, and the siren sounds in the distance which is the signal for the men to embark.

"Let's go!"

They mount the gangway. In 15 minutes all is ready. The two generals head up the gangway, and I come with them. Ganay turns to look not at his inferiors, but friends, and his voice quavers as he addresses them:

"Goodbye, guys! I wish I were in your boots. (He smiles and looks at the men crowding the quai.) So, who wants to trade places with me?"

"Bibi here, Sir!"

Ganay looks over to see a young blond soldier hoisted onto the shoulders of the others. This gives the general a smile, but he murmurs with a touch of bitterness:

"You don't know what you'll be losing yet, kid. Your hair and your youth."

Out on the calm sea the sky is clear. The ship skims along like a gull. Captain Lamarque with his brilliant blue eyes walks down the passageway reading the *Red Lily* by Anatole France. The men are leaning on the rails and all nations are present: Germans, Austrians, and Swiss form one group, Belgians form another, and Spaniards a third. A lone Greek does not know who to talk to, so his fingers wander over the holes of his fife.

Most play cards while reclining on empty sacks and blankets. I see one sitting on a plank reading an issue of *Temperance.* An energetic little man with a bushy mustache points to the legionnaire:

"Look at this one. He's a Czech who can't read French. If he knew the name of the magazine he was holding he'd chuck it overboard. He spent two weeks in the can last month for drunkenness."

A lieutenant takes me to the canteen where we meet some friends.

I ask: "What do you guys do after Marseille?"

"We all embark on the *Natal* on the 10th and get to Majunga on the 1st of January. Majunga is the base. The core of the battalion has a captain-major, a detail officer and three secretaries, as well as a noncom."

"And once there?"

"The officer designated by general Gallieni will give us our orders. First we'll go out to relieve the outposts. There are 4 main posts, and each gets one company. Then they will form four reinforcement teams from the rest of the detachment."

"Where will they go?"

"A coastal ferry will take them to different camps on the west coast up to Tulear, and the team destined for Fort-Dauphin will go to Tamatave to will be sent to a camp with less chance of plague."

"Shit." says one officer, "There's more plague in Paris than in Madagascar."

"And once you're at your posts?"

"We arrive there, pass along orders, and the men and officers who have already done their tour will head back to the coast and meet up at Majunga, where they will head back to France. Relief accomplished."

One officer says to another:

"Is your shopping list for Marseille all ready?"

"Yes."

I read the list over his shoulder:

To purchase: skillet, grill, plates (one case),
Vichy salts, magnifying glass, machete, mosquito

netting, portable compass alidade, vegetable seeds,
camera, boot polish, salt, pipe, striker, petrole lamp,
hunting rifle, maps, quinine, cocaine, caffeine,
morphine, ether, iodine, salol, suppositories,
thermometer, smelling salts, etc.

I have to smile behind my hand when I read:

Hypodermic needle for the clap.

"You forgot a botany manual," someone adds,
"sometimes a sector commandant has to give a
course on the local flora."

"And a barometric thermometer."

"No way. Three Louis is too much."

"An alarm clock."

"Ha! You don't sleep over there. Besides I've
been to the colonies, and you need to pack light. But
you have to know a bit of everything, and if I could I
would buy the memory of a genius. Colombat is

located 27 klics from the nearest telegraph post. Pass me the notebook. Cheers!"

I go out and stroll on up to the bridge. Captain Lamarque is sitting there reading the *Red Lily.* There are many people who think that guys in the legion don't read.

"Do you think there will be fighting over there?"

The lieutenant I am asking smiles:

"I hope so. The action is going on in the southwest, the wildest part of Madagascar, from the river Tsihiribina south to Majunga up to Fort Dauphin. This country is classed as desert on the maps since it lacks any kind of surface water, but no one knows for sure. That's why they send in Legionnaires."

Beside us some men are eating. Tonight the dish is *l'olla podrida:* vermicelli, beans, chickpeas.

3 officers and 150 men left for Madagascar in June of 1898, 3 officers for Vietnam on the 1st of July, 7 officers and 950 men for Vietnam on the 1st of September, 9 officers and 240 men for Madagascar on the 10th of December, and as it was necessary to send 500 men and 3 officers to Vietnam on the 1st of January, that makes for two regiments alone 1,840 men and 25 officers in just 6 months. How many will come back? Eat up legionnaires, you'll never get this much sustenance in the colonies. And the fever and the indigenous personnel are waiting to eat you alive.

A serene night comes down. I climb down to the hold where everyone is asleep. Not a motion, not a sound. Mysterious men, rebels beaten down, rejects of nations, living regrets for far-off mothers. Sleep well, oh beaten men of the world, and dream of the glorious death you desire, forgotten…

I leave on tiptoe.

Marseille appears. Captain Lamarque closes the *Red Lily* for debarkment and goodbyes.

"So," I say to lieutenant C… who is already decorated, "Goodbye and good look. Come back with more medals."

"Shit! Do you know what I'll bring back for sure, if I make it?"

"A promotion?"

"Liver trouble and a bad attitude!" he says with a grin, "Plus three years of malaria and anemia – but some damn good stories."

One of the porters on the train grabs my bags and I'm off for Paris.

Before rolling away I can see the ship there under its plume of smoke as it heads off, and meditating upon all of the things I have seen, my heart becomes heavy. Those men on that boat-- what can they be sure of in this life? The smoke of the ship's stack is the perfect image for them, rolling up and disappearing, for what? What drives them on and up? The ship moves off. I must not pity them. They are full of courage and devotion beyond words. Besides smoke rises up and up and becomes like the lumenous air at last, mounting skyward like a prayer, rising up like the undying part of all men.

Credo, Credo, Credo!

A post in Madagascar.

END.

Printed in Great Britain
by Amazon